THE CORK COOK BOOK

acknowledgements

This book is dedicated to Cork Simon, a community where people can grow and develop as human beings.

The Cork Simon Community would sincerely like to thank the following people who helped to make this book possible:

The Loyola Foundation who grant aided the project.

All the restaurants and establishments for their contributions and support.

John and Sally McKenna for their contributions and encouragement throughout this project.

Myrtle Allen for her contribution and support.

Dick Shannon of the Simon Community National Office for his introduction.

Darina Allen and Michael Ryan for their helpful suggestions.

The Ballincollig Irish Country Women's Association (ICA) who tested the recipes.

Fuji Photo Film Ireland Ltd. for their sponsorship, providing Fuji film for all the photographs in this publication.

Jackie Brown at Primary Colour for sponsoring all the colour processing of the photographs.

Ann Farrell for fund-raising and seeing the project through to completion.

To Nuala Fenton, Angie Shanahan and Damhnait Sweeney for collating and editing the introductions and recipes.

Special thanks also to: Patricia McAllister (Director of the Cork Simon Community), Marion McAuliffe, Kathleen Boyle, Clarie O'Leary, Robert South, Regina Sexton, Kieran and Sylvia from Upper Case, Kyle Cathie Ltd., Colleen O'Sullivan, Penny Wray, Hilary O'Kelly, Eileen Singleton and Grace McDonagh.

Photography by Michael O'Toole

Food Styling by Ann Marie Tobin

Design by Cobalt Design, Kevin Gurry, Brendan McCarthy and Melina Taylor

Printed by Nicholson and Bass

Editors:

Nuala Fenton
Angie Shanahan
Damhnait Sweeney

Project Co-ordinators:

Ann Farrell
Rachel Stevens

A.N
641.5

about the cork simon community

Since 1971, Cork Simon Community has been providing a wide range of services to homeless people. These services include a soup run, shelter, residential houses, referral and settlement support, a crafts project, a shop and a social club.

But Cork Simon is much more than a provider of essential services. The Simon Community is about working and campaigning for justice in a practical way. It is about community, solidarity and respect for the dignity of the individual. For many homeless people, the Simon Community is about a meal, a bed for the night and human companionship. For some it is home. For many others it is a point of contact. It is a place where people work. It is an opportunity for volunteers to give of themselves, their time and their talents. Above all, Simon is about community where people can grow and develop as human beings.

In addition to its activities at local level, Cork Simon Community works closely with the Simon Communities in Dublin, Dundalk and Galway and together they make up the Simon Community of Ireland, which is the national federation.

The work of the Simon Community is carried out by full-time and part-time volunteers, staff, and a number of people employed under the Community Employment Scheme administered by FÁS. Most of the funding required to manage and run Cork Simon's services and projects is raised by the Community itself through voluntary fundraising such as flag days, church gate collections, the Simon shop and sponsored events. Without the generosity and support of the people of Cork and surrounding counties, it would not have been possible for Cork Simon to develop its work with homeless people over the years.

More and more money is needed to run existing projects and to develop new and innovative services for homeless people. This Cook Book is being published to raise funds for Cork Simon's work. I should like to pay tribute to everyone involved in its planning, preparation and production. A special word of thanks to all the restaurants which contributed the recipes and the Loyola Foundation for its generous grant to finance this very worthwhile project.

Dick Shannon
National Director

introduction

You will never be at a loss when thinking of places to eat out in Cork. The variety and quality of the city and county restaurants makes living here or visiting the area such a pleasure.

Cork's reputation for fine food has grown steadily over the past twenty years, from the high standards set by establishments such as Ballymaloe, the Arbutus Lodge Hotel and organisations such as the "Kinsale Good Food Circle". The emphasis has always been on the use of fresh,locally grown produce and exacting standards in training. This, combined with good business acumen, has contributed enormously to the development of Cork's reputation as a centre for excellent food.

Featured here is a selection of culinary ideas from many of Cork's most talented chefs. Our aim with this book is to express their creativity and individuality of approach and to show the extraordinary vitality in the best of Cork food today. This compilation is drawn from thirty different establishments, ranging from bistro-style restaurants to country houses. When inviting contributions, we did not insist on each section being a set menu, therefore many of the recipes can be used as starters or main courses. The thread running through this book is an emphasis on quality, fresh ingredients, used in season. These can be sourced in local country markets, good quality shops, supermarkets, from organic suppliers or if you are in Cork city, at the English Market in Princes Street.

A book which would highlight the culinary genius of Cork has been an obvious project for some time. We also wanted a project which would raise funds for the Cork Simon Community, which takes such an essential responsibility within the city. The chefs and contributors were particularly delighted to be involved with a project for Simon and gladly gave of their time for it. We hope that you will enjoy cooking from this book.

Nuala Fenton, Angie Shanahan, Damhnait Sweeney (Editors)

cork food — past and present

Cork Food in the Past by Myrtle Allen

There are certain everyday things that are virtually never written about - so commonplace that, at the time, it is unimaginable that anyone should be curious about them. Artefacts survive but foods, flavours and textures, are utterly ephemeral, so it is very hard to get an idea of Cork food in the past. Much easier for me to recall is the food of Cork in the first half of this century. This was the era of the great family firms where a name was at stake, in addition to the essential bottom line of profit. Here are the highlights of my childhood, a sort of, 'Good Food Guide to Cork' 1930 edition!

In the 1930's two of my favourite shops could be found on MacCurtain or King's Street,

Thompson's and Hadji Bey. Thompson's had large, shell shaped meringues, crisp on the outside, slightly soft and moist in the middle. They were to be filled with whipped cream at home. Thompson's was also best known for its brown bread, 'Thoma' loaf and their white bread 'Duck'. Other recommended confections included Lemon Buns, London Buns, and Barm Brack. Hadji Bey specialised in Turkish Delight, boxes of chocolates, chocolate bars, figures and animals. Pembroke Street and St. Patrick's Street was blessed with Cudmores who provided fresh fruit and vegetables from the big private gardens of the country. There were big juicy black grapes, imported and home grown as well as home

grown plums and greengages. Their window displays were colourful, elongated pyramids of fruit. Bunches of wild watercress and cream cheeses sold in silver paper packets could be found in Russell's on Princes Street. This street was also home for O'Donovan's bacon, ham and poultry and they are still trading today. In the market one could find prime meats from Mr Barrel, Mr Waugh and Mr O'Flynn. Of places to eat and drink,

Thompson's of Prince's Street provided delicious cakes, buns and strawberry ice-cream. The most exclusive Drinking Club was on St. Patrick's Street, The Cubbyhole, behind Smith's Stores. It was very tiny, and very dark with benches down each wall, and a table

Cork Food Today by John McKenna

squeezed into the middle. The walls were lined with bottles and it was Men Only (except for me with my grandfather). Many of the gentlemen there were tasting with a view to buying, as well as just drinking. They were overseen by the proprietor, old Mr Smith with his long white beard. The Pavilion Cinema Restaurant, also on St. Patrick's Street, had a cold meat buffet table. The Oyster Tavern on Market Lane was not for children, and how one longed to be old enough and rich enough to join the smart young set there. Steaks were cooked in the restaurant on an open fire grill and it had such a cosy bar.

Excellent food can be found in Cork now, but this was also true in the past.

Cork is the cauldron of good food in Ireland, the place where the fire of the kitchens and the hunger of the people ignite to create pleasure. The parallel paths of creative cooking and confident appreciation run side-by-side throughout the county.

More than anywhere else in Ireland, the chefs and cooks of County Cork exhibit a hunger for the new, the challenging and the sublime. Above all, they demonstrate all the virtues of a 'can do' mentality, with each new adventure eagerly seized upon, each new avenue of food eagerly explored and enjoyed.

A love of good things is deep rooted in the psyche of Cork people. This appreciation has been quickly acquired and adopted by the many people who have come to live in the county over the last two decades many of whom have, in their own right, become cooks and food producers.

The attitude of the people of the county is truly Mediterranean in spirit, and they are comfortable with the enjoyment of life, quick to discover and appreciate the good things. They are fortunate to have so many fine cooks actively creating a contemporary food culture all around them, inquisitively moving our experiences of exciting cooking ever forward.

12

contents

cork

city

"When trying to decide which recipes to offer up here, I initially searched through all the chaotic collections of scribblings and lists we call 'recipe books' in the café, looking for the most impressive, the technically challenging ones that use frightening quantities of expensive ingredients. But it was late July, the beginning of the harvest of sun-ripened vegetables; a brilliant time of year to be involved with vegetables, and a time when the produce is so wonderful in its own right that a cook's simple job is to get it to the table with its inherent pleasure-giving qualities intact. Take a sun-ripened organic tomato, halve it, tear a small basil leaf over it, season it and drizzle some fine olive oil over each half. The sensual pleasure

16

aubergine, tomato, olive and goat's cheese galette, page 19

available from this delicacy can't be conjured up, faked or replicated by the most technically talented cook unless he/she starts with the sun ripened organic tomato in the first place.

These are the glory days, when the growers and suppliers come in beaming with pride. Late summer is the easiest time to be a vegetarian cook, when the menus are practically dictated by the vegetables and the people who grow them. In the food cultures we admire, the focus of admiration is much more on the quality of the foods grown and produced than on the dishes prepared by the cooks. Growers, here, of fine vegetables, are perceived still as eccentric, foolhardy, probably foreign, and, by those of us who need them, heroic." Denis Cotter

broad bean, new potato & roasted beetroot salad
with a walnut dressing and orla shavings

SERVES 4

VEGETABLES
4 medium sized beetroots
200 g (7 oz) new potatoes
160 g (5½ oz) broad beans
(weight with pods removed)

SALAD
2 medium heads of lettuce (use one or
two types of lollo rosso, frisée, oakleaf,
cos, and some fresh fennel and
dill herb sprigs, if possible)
2 scallions, finely sliced

DRESSING
250 ml (8 fluid oz)
extra virgin olive oil
50 ml (1½ fluid oz) walnut oil
50 ml (1½ fluid oz) balsamic vinegar
2 cloves of garlic,
peeled and crushed
salt and freshly ground
pepper to taste

TO FINISH
extra virgin olive oil for
roasting the beetroot
50 g (2 oz) Orla cheese,
or similar

Leave about 5 cm (2 in) of leaf stalks on top and most of the root on the beet. Wash well under cold running water, taking care not to damage the skin, otherwise the beetroot will bleed during cooking. Cover with cold water, bring to the boil, reduce the heat and simmer gently until just cooked - this should take about half an hour, but can take much longer if the roots are old and stubborn. Under cold water, rub off the outer skin with your fingers - if it doesn't rub away easily, curse a little and take a knife to them.

Dressing
Meanwhile, make the dressing by whisking together the oils, vinegar, garlic and seasoning in a bowl. Leave aside.

Vegetables
Preheat the oven to 230°C/450°F/gas mark 7.
Scrub the potatoes and cut into slices 5 mm (1/4 in) thick and cook them in boiling salted water until just tender. Cool them a little with cold running water and drain, then toss them in enough dressing to coat each slice. Cook and dress the broad beans in the same way. Slice each of the beetroots into six wedges, toss these in enough olive oil to coat them, place on a baking tray and roast in the preheated oven, turning once or twice, until the outside of the roots begin to caramelise (about 10 minutes).

Salad
Meanwhile, tear the washed lettuce into large bite-size pieces and place in a large salad bowl. Add the scallions, broad beans, potatoes, fennel, salt and freshly ground pepper and toss with enough dressing to coat everything lightly.

To serve
Divide the salad between 4 plates, keeping an eye on the distribution of the starring vegetables. Take the beetroot from the oven and arrange six wedges on each plate. Finally, using a potato peeler, scatter thin shavings of the cheese generously and randomly over the salad.

aubergine, tomato, olive and goat's cheese galette
with a balsamic-tomato vinaigrette

4 small aubergines or 3 medium
30 ml (1 fluid oz) olive oil
8 tomatoes
300 g (11 oz) goat's cheese
about 4 tablespoons of olive tapenade
freshly ground black pepper

VINAIGRETTE
2 cloves of garlic, crushed
500 ml (16 fluid oz) olive oil
150 ml (5 fluid oz) tomato passata
(use a good quality tomato
purée not concentrated)
100 ml (3 fluid oz) balsamic vinegar
salt and freshly ground pepper

Preheat the oven to 230°C/450°F/gas mark 7.

Galette
Preparation
Shave a slice off the aubergines lengthways to remove the rounded outer edges. This will enable the slices to sit flat on the baking tray. Then, cut each aubergine into four fairly thin slices. Brush both sides with olive oil and roast in the preheated oven for 10-15 minutes, turning once if necessary.
Slice the tomatoes very thinly and de-seed them.
Slice the cheese thinly also, but if it won't co-operate, finely crumbled will do.
Assembly
Spread a thin scraping of tapenade on a slice of aubergine, and top that with an even layer of tomato, freshly ground black pepper, then a layer of cheese. Press another slice of aubergine on top of this, and repeat the process until you have three layers of filling and four of aubergine. Repeat to make three more cakes. Adjust the oven temperature to 180°C/350°F/gas mark 4.
Place the cakes on an oven tray and bake for about twenty minutes. Check them occasionally to avoid overcooking - you can lose a lot of the cheese if you forget them!

Vinaigrette
Crush the garlic and place it in a jug with the other ingredients. Using a strong hand liquidiser, blend the sauce into an emulsified, thickened consistency. Taste and check the flavour for balance - you may need to adjust one or all the components. Leave aside and whisk well before using.

To serve
Serve one galette per person, with a little of the vinaigrette poured around it.
To accompany - I usually serve this with fried or grilled polenta, or a little risotto, or new potatoes if you are an addict, and some lightly cooked greens - chard, kale, beans, spinach, mangetout - whatever you've got in that pristine little vegetable patch I know you've all got out the back there!

gooseberry - almond tartlets
with an amaretto custard

SERVES 8

Preheat the oven to 175°C/350°F/gas mark 4.

PASTRY
80 g (3 oz) unsalted butter
80 g (3 oz) caster sugar
80 g (3 oz) ground almonds

Pastry
Cream the butter, almonds and 80 g (3 oz) of caster sugar. Lightly butter eight shallow tartlet tins (or Yorkshire pudding trays). Put one rounded dessertspoon of the pastry in each and flatten it slightly with the back of the spoon, but don't attempt to shape it into the tin in any serious way. The pastry will rise a little in the baking and collapse to form a shallow lipped base. Bake the pastries for 20-25 minutes, until lightly browned, then leave them to cool in the trays.

FILLING
600 g (1 lb) gooseberries
400 g (14 oz) caster sugar

Filling
Meanwhile, place the gooseberries and the 400 g (14 oz) of caster sugar in a heavy pan and cook them very gently over a very low heat, until the gooseberries have softened but still hold their shape. Tip the gooseberries and their syrup into a bowl and leave them to cool to room temperature.

APRICOT GLAZE
100 g (3½oz) apricot jam
1 teaspoon lemon juice
1 tablespoon water

Glaze
The apricot glaze needs to be warm and thickly pourable, so make it now and warm it up when you need it, or do it just before serving. Simply heat the jam, lemon juice and water together in a pan until pourable, then sieve the result.

CUSTARD
3 egg yolks
70g (3 oz) caster sugar
300 ml (10 fluid oz) cream
1 tablespoon Amaretto liqueur

Amaretto custard
This custard recipe is recommended to serve with the Gooseberry & Almond Tarlets, but it is a lovely custard which can complement many desserts.

Whisk the egg yolks and caster sugar together until fluffy. In a pan, heat the cream gently, but do not boil. Pour the cream over the egg and sugar, stir in gently and return the lot to the pan with the Amaretto liqueur. Now, heat the custard very gently, stirring all the time, until it has thickened to a good pouring consistency. Fans of extra-thick custard will risk curdling the eggs if they go on too long in search of their goal.

Café Paradiso, Washington Street, Cork City

The custard is at it's best if left to cool to lukewarm, but can also be used hot, cold, or even carefully reheated.

To serve
Remove the pastries from their tins (very carefully as they're quite fragile) and place them on plates. Spoon a generous pile of gooseberries into each pastry, and brush a thin layer of glaze over each pile. Pour a small pool of custard onto the plates and put the jug on the table for the custard freaks to indulge their cravings!

deep fried chicken
with milleens cheese on red onion marmalade

SERVES 4

2 large chicken breasts,
roughly chopped
60 ml (2 fluid oz) fresh cream
1 egg white
pinch of nutmeg
salt and freshly ground
black pepper

TO ASSEMBLE

2 tablespoons of flour seasoned
with salt and freshly ground pepper
160 g (5½ oz) Irish Milleens Cheese
divided into four
egg wash (1 egg whisked
with 4 tablespoons of milk)
80 g (3 oz) white breadcrumbs

RED ONION MARMALADE

2 large red onions,
finely chopped
100g (3½ oz) brown sugar
15 ml (½ fluid oz) water
2 tablespoons of Irish honey
350 ml (12 fluid oz) red wine
125 ml (4 fluid oz) white
wine vinegar
1 teaspoon of finely chopped
fresh coriander
salt and freshly ground black pepper

Preparing the chicken
Put the chopped chicken in a liquidiser and process in
an on/off method until the chicken is finely chopped.
Set aside.

Put the the egg white into a bowl along with the
nutmeg, finely chopped chicken and seasoning.
Cautiously, add just enough of the cream to make a not
too soft consistency.
Mix well and divide into four portions.

Shape the mixture into four balls using seasoned flour.
Conceal a portion of Milleens cheese in the centre of
each ball.
Brush with the egg wash and toss in the breadcrumbs.
Leave aside.

Red onion marmalade
Put the wine, wine vinegar, water, sugar and honey into
a heavy based stainless steel saucepan.
Bring to the boil and add the finely chopped red onions.
Lower the heat and simmer for 10 minutes.
Add the fresh coriander and season to taste with salt
and freshly ground black pepper.

To cook the chicken
Fry the chicken in a deep fat fryer for approximately
2 minutes until lightly crisp and golden.
Drain on kitchen paper.

To serve
Spoon a little of the red onion marmalade into the centre
of four warmed plates. Cut each of the chicken balls in
half and arrange on top of the marmalade.
Serve immediately.

clonakilty black pudding
with a stew of wild rice, pearl barley and mushrooms

SERVES 4

THE STEW

75 g (3 oz) pearl barley

75 g (3 oz) black wild rice

600 ml (1 pint) good home-made
chicken stock (reserve 2 tablespoons)

2 bay leaves

2 sprigs of thyme

2 cloves of garlic

a knob of butter

25 g (1 oz) olive oil

salt and freshly ground black pepper

THE MUSHROOMS AND PUDDING

25g (1 oz) butter

75g (3 oz) wild mushrooms

100g (3½ oz) black pudding, sliced

Soak the pearl barley and wild rice in separate bowls of cold water for three hours. Drain and rinse.

Put the rice, half the chicken stock, a bay leaf with a sprig of thyme and a clove of garlic in a saucepan, bring to the boil, reduce the heat and simmer gently for 20 minutes. Put the barley in a separate saucepan and follow the same procedure as above except cook for only 10 minutes. When both are cooked, remove from the heat and do not drain. Remove the thyme, bay leaf and garlic from each pan and discard.
Mix the wild rice with the pearl barley and add the two tablespoons of reserved chicken stock, a knob of butter and the olive oil. Season to taste with salt and freshly ground black pepper.

To cook the mushrooms and pudding
Melt the butter in a large frying pan. Sauté the wild mushrooms for 2-3 minutes, remove and keep warm. In the same pan, cook the slices of black pudding on both sides until heated through. Don't allow them to get too crusty on the outside.

To serve
Divide the rice and pearl barley between four warmed soup bowls. Arrange the slices of black pudding on top and scatter the mushrooms around. Serve immediately.

clonakilty black pudding with a stew of
wild rice, pearl barley and mushrooms

"Make it simple and use the very best ingredients you can get of their kind. This could mean a superbly made black pudding or a neck of the tenderest lamb - or at another level, the fattest freshest liver of Strasbourg goose."

Chef Michael Clifford has been an important influence on contemporary Irish cooking as well as having a major impact on the culinary life of Cork over the past decade.

spinach and mushroom pancakes
with hollandaise sauce

SERVES 6

PANCAKE BATTER
makes approx. 12
175 g (6 oz) white flour
pinch of salt
3 free range eggs, lightly beaten
275 ml (½ pint) milk and 150 ml
(¼ pint) water mixed together (sparkling
water if you have it)
2-3 tablespoons of olive oil

MUSHROOM À LA CRÈME
25 g (1 oz) butter
175 g (6 oz) onion, finely chopped
450 g (1 lb) button mushrooms, sliced
240 ml (8 fluid oz) cream
small piece of roux
1 tablespoon of chopped parsley
squeeze of lemon juice
salt and freshly ground pepper
125 g (4 oz) cooked, chopped spinach

HOLLANDAISE SAUCE
2 egg yolks
1 dessertspoon of cold water
125 g (4 oz) butter
2 teaspoons of lemon juice
salt and freshly ground white pepper

Sieve the flour and salt into a bowl, make a well in the centre and drop in the lightly beaten eggs. Starting in the centre, using a whisk, mix the egg and gradually draw in the flour. Add the liquid slowly and beat until the batter is covered with bubbles. Let the batter stand in a cold place for an hour or so.
Just before you cook the pancakes stir in the oil.

Mushroom à la crème
Melt the butter in a heavy bottomed saucepan until it begins to foam. Add the finely chopped onion, cover and sweat over a gentle heat until soft but not coloured.
Meanwhile, heat a little butter or oil in a hot frying pan and cook the sliced mushrooms in batches. Season each batch with salt, freshly ground pepper and a squeeze of lemon juice.
Add the mushrooms to the onions in the saucepan, pour in the cream and allow to bubble gently for a few minutes. Thicken slightly with a little roux.
Add a squeeze of lemon juice, the chopped parsley and the cooked spinach and heat through. Taste and adjust seasoning if necessary.

Hollandaise sauce
Put the egg yolks into a heavy based stainless steel saucepan over a very gentle heat. Add the cold water and whisk thoroughly. Gradually, add the butter, piece by piece, whisking all the time until the sauce begins to thicken to a heavy cream. If it seems to be thickening too quickly or even suggests a scrambling quality, immediately remove from the heat and add a little cold water. Do not stop whisking until the sauce is made. Finally add the lemon juice and season to taste with salt and freshly ground pepper.
Hollandaise sauce is served warm, not hot. If it is kept too warm it will thin out or curdle. It can be held perfectly for an hour or more in a pan of lukewarm water.

spinach and mushroom pancakes with hollandaise sauce

To cook the pancakes
Heat a non-stick frying pan, 20 cm (8 in) in diameter, over a high heat. Pour in a small ladle full of batter, just enough to lightly cover the base of the pan. When golden, turn or flip the pancake over and cook for a few seconds on the other side. Slide onto a plate and keep warm while you cook the others.

To serve
Lay a pancake on a clean plate. Put about 2 tablespoons of filling in the centre, and roll the pancake into a cylinder. Repeat with the others. Arrange two pancakes per person on six warmed plates. Spoon over a little of the Hollandaise sauce and serve with a good green salad.

fantailed potatoes
with rosemary and garlic

SERVES 4

4 medium potatoes
8 cloves of garlic cut into slivers
8 sprigs of rosemary
125 g (4 oz) of clarified butter
salt and freshly ground black pepper

Preheat the oven to 230°C/450°F/gas mark 7.

To clarify the butter
It is best to use unsalted butter for this task. Remember that about 20 per cent of the volume of butter is lost in clarifying. The exact proportion depends on the quality of the butter, therefore always clarify more butter than the recipe requests.
Cut the butter into pieces, put it into a pan and bring it to a good, bubbling boil. Remove from the heat and allow to settle.
Meanwhile wring out a double thickness of muslin in hot water and use it to line a sieve. Set the sieve over a small bowl and carefully ladle the melted butter into the lined sieve. The muslin will retain any white milk solids; discard these and keep the cooled butter covered in the refrigerator until ready to use.

To cook the potatoes
Wash and peel the potatoes and dry thoroughly with kitchen paper.
Coat each potato with clarified butter. Cut several slits in each potato and insert the garlic slivers and the rosemary sprigs. Place on a baking tray and season with salt and freshly ground pepper.
Bake in the preheated oven for 40-50 minutes.

medallions of venison with redcurrants,
braised red cabbage and fantailed potatoes,
with rosemary and garlic

SERVES 4

12 medallions of venison
each weighing approx. 40 g (1¾ oz)
25 g (1 oz) butter
1 tablespoon of olive oil
salt and freshly ground pepper

SAUCE

2 tablespoons of red wine
2 tablespoons of red wine vinegar
575 ml (1 pint) of good venison stock
1 bay leaf
3 peppercorns
4 tablespoons of fresh or frozen redcurrants
(frozen redcurrants may
require a sprinkling of sugar)

RED CABBAGE

450 g (1 lb) red cabbage
(Red Drummond if possible)
450 g (1 lb) cooking apples
(Bramley Seedling)
1 tablespoon of wine vinegar
120 ml (4 fluid oz) water
1 level teaspoon of salt
1 heaped tablespoon of sugar

Venison
Season the venison with salt and freshly ground pepper. Heat the oil and butter in a heavy based frying pan over a high heat and sear the medallions for 1 minute on each side, or to your taste.
Remove to a plate and keep warm.

Sauce
Pour the excess fat from the pan, then return the pan to the heat, pour in the wine and the wine vinegar. Turn up the heat and stirring briskly with a wooden spoon, scrape the base and sides of the pan to release the coagulated meat juices.
Bring the liquid to the boil and allow it to evaporate.
Stir in the venison stock, the bay leaf and the peppercorns.
Bring to the boil and reduce to a light coating consistency.
Add the red currants to the sauce and heat through for a few seconds.
Taste, season with salt and freshly ground black pepper and a little sugar if necessary. Keep warm.

To serve
Have ready four warmed plates.
Arrange 3 medallions of venison on each plate and spoon over the hot sauce. Serve immediately with a side dish of red cabbage and a fantailed potato with rosemary and garlic.

Red Cabbage
Remove any damaged outer leaves from the cabbage.
Examine and clean it if necessary. Cut into quarters, remove the core and slice the cabbage finely across the grain.
Put the wine vinegar, water, salt and sugar into a cast iron or stainless steel saucepan. Add the cabbage and bring it to the boil.
Meanwhile, peel and core the apples and cut into quarters (no smaller). Lay them on top of the cabbage, cover and continue to cook gently until the cabbage is tender, approximately 30-50 minutes. Do not overcook or the colour and flavour will be ruined. Taste for seasoning and add more sugar if necessary.

To serve
Turn into a warmed serving dish and serve with the medallions of venison.

Set up by Ballymaloe in the Crawford Art Gallery, Cork, the café is located in a building which dates from 1724. It houses an important art collection, some of which may be enjoyed in the café surroundings. Here you can tuck into a delicous lunch or afternoon coffee and cake, happy in the knowledge that your needs will be attended to by the efficent waitressing staff. Chef Chris O'Brien maintains the high Ballymaloe standard.

brioche des clochards

MAKES 10

"This recipe follows a folklore tradition of putting one thing in your pocket which will sustain you (the true reason for pockets!) - perhaps as you are stalking urchins!!!"

DOUGH
20 g (¾ oz) fresh yeast
120 ml (4 fluid oz) of tepid milk
10 g (½ oz) salt
50 g (2 oz) sugar
500 g (18 oz) strong white flour
4 eggs, beaten
300 g (11 oz) softened butter

PATÉ
1 large onion, peeled, and finely chopped
2 cloves of garlic, peeled and crushed
a sprig each of rosemary, parsley and thyme

500 g (18 oz) duck, goose or 'happy farm' chicken livers
250 ml (8 fluid oz) duck or goose fat (or butter)
a pinch of sugar

2 egg yolks
300 g (11 oz) butter
salt and freshly ground black pepper

200 g (7 oz) raisins soaked in whiskey overnight

Brioche dough
Pour the tepid milk into a measuring jug, add the yeast and let it dissolve. Then, stir in the salt and sugar and leave aside to liquefy completely. Sieve the flour into a mixing bowl, make a well in the centre, add the eggs and the yeast mixture.
Cut and mix everything together with a rubber spatula to form a dough. Turn out onto a lightly floured kneading surface and let the dough rest for 2-3 minutes.
Knead by lifting, folding, slapping, and pushing with the heel of your hand. If the dough remains sticky, knead in a tablespoon or so more flour. When it becomes smooth and elastic, begin working in the butter. Taking small pieces, start rapidly folding and smearing the butter into the dough with the heel of your hand, then gather the dough into a mass and smear again. Keep working in more bits of butter as each previous addition is partially absorbed, always using the heel of your hand and cutting with the spatula. Continue until all the butter is incorporated.
Place the dough in a bowl, put the bowl into a plastic bag, cover with a towel and place at a temperature of 68-72°F.
Leave to rise for 2-3 hours. When the dough has risen to 3½ times its original volume, knead again to deflate and dispel accumulated gas. Refrigerate for 2 hours.

Liver Paté
Heat the fat or butter in a saucepan over a medium heat. Add the onions, garlic and herbs and fry until golden and aromatic.
Transfer to the bowl of a food processor.
In the same pan, fry the livers until slightly firm, sprinkle with a pinch of sugar, turn over and cook until medium rare. Place in the food processor along with the onion - garlic mixture and blend until smooth. Add the egg yolks and beat in the butter, little by little until all is well incorporated. Season to taste with salt and freshly ground pepper and refrigerate until needed.

For chef Seamus O' Connell, the day starts with a check of what is available in the local market before he sets to work creating.

"He is a culinary polymath who simply works in a parallel universe to every other cook in the country: the other guys are doing landscapes with trees and horses whilst Seamus is tearing the canvas apart with cubism."

(John McKenna, 100 best Restaurants in Ireland, 1998)

Forming the paté en brioche
On a lightly floured board, roll out the dough into a 2 cm (¾ in) thick rectangle, measuring 50 cm x 25 cm (20 in x 10 in). Spread the paté over the dough, and sprinkle on the raisins. Roll up into a roulade, slice at 5 cm (2 in) intervals and place the rounds flat on a lightly oiled baking tray, like a Danish pastry. Leave to rise for 1 hour at room temperature.
Preheat the oven to 190°C/375°F/gas mark 5.
Bake in the preheated oven for 20-30 minutes. Remove and cool on a wire rack. Perfect for slummy picnics!!

Note: Variation
You could also, put a layer of chopped, raw goose liver, or cooked ham on top of the paté before you roll the roulade.

sea urchin consommé with gyoza

"This dish may seem far fetched and tedious but it is quite fun really (if you can get urchins), and the effect of such a sublime flavour, with the black urchin like dumplings lurking in the depths of such clarity is as worth the effort as anything else. If you like, you can make it with mussels, replicating the shape of said crustacean with like effect." Seamus O'Connell

Sea Urchins are best when there is an 'r' in the month.

900 g (2 lb) large prawns (preferably live)
4-6 sea urchins

STOCK
prawn shells
sea urchin shells
1 tablespoon of vegetable oil
2 litres of fish stock or water
1 small carrot, scraped and cut into dice
1 small onion, peeled and finely chopped
the peel from 2 cloves of garlic
1 teaspoon of tomato pureé
450 g (1 lb) fresh spinach, washed

GYOZA
"These are traditional Chinese or Korean dumplings, usually filled with pork or prawns, leeks and cabbage, then fried on one side and steamed on the other. Locally, they are best enjoyed while watching sumo wrestling!"

Preparation
Shell and devein the prawns, wash well and pat dry with kitchen paper. Reserve the shells. To prepare the sea urchins, scrape the prickles from the top of the shell. Lever out the plug with the end of a teaspoon or point of a kitchen scissors. Cut a large hole at the top of each urchin and remove the roe (coral). Reserve the shells.

Stock
Heat the olive oil in a large stockpot until quite hot. Add the prawn shells and sauté until well browned. Pour in the fish stock or water and add the sea urchin shells, the diced carrot, onion, and garlic peels. Bring to the boil, lower the heat and simmer gently for 30 minutes. Finally, stir in the tomato pureé and strain the stock through a fine sieve into a clean saucepan. Leave aside. Remove approximately 575 ml (1 pint) of the stock into a separate saucepan. Bring to the boil and blanch the spinach for 10 seconds. Drain and refresh under cold running water, drain again and squeeze dry. Reserve.

Gyoza
To make the dough - combine the ink, water and salt in a jug and mix well with a fork. Sieve the flour into a bowl and make a well in the centre.
Pour the ink mixture into the well and using a whisk, gradually draw in all the flour until you have a stiff paste. Dust some flour onto the work top and knead the dough (incorporating a little more flour if necessary) until you achieve the texture of an earlobe or, in better known terms, until the dough becomes smooth and elastic and begins to clean itself off the working surface. Set aside.

DOUGH
200 g (7 oz) white flour
I sachet of squid ink
50 ml (2 fluid oz) water
a pinch of salt

FILLING
the prepared prawns
the cooked spinach
I bunch of spring onions
2 leaves of basil
the urchin roes
2 cloves of garlic,
(reserved from above) crushed
I egg yolk
salt and freshly ground pepper

TO COAT THE GYOZA
dusting flour for rolling out
2 egg yolks, beaten
225 g (8 oz) black fine noodles, broken or
nouillettes if you can get them
vegetable oil for deep-frying the gyoza

CONSOMMÉ
the stock
salt and freshly ground pepper
I pinch of cinnamon
6 egg whites
I tablespoon of white wine vinegar

GARNISH
reserved white parts of scallions, finely
chopped

To make the filling - chop the prawns, the urchin roes and the spinach finely and put into a bowl.

Mince the green section of the spring onions (reserving the white part for the garnish) and the garlic very finely and toss these into the bowl too. Add the egg yolk, the salt and freshly ground pepper and mix thoroughly.

On a lightly floured work top, roll out the dough to about 5 mm (¼ in) thick and using a plain pastry cutter, cut out 8 circles measuring 9 cm (3½ in) in diameter. With a pastry brush, brush the outer edges with cold water. Place 1 tablespoon of prawn mixture in the centre and fold over to form a purse shape, pinching off any excess dough.

Repeat this procedure to make a further eight purses. Brush each purse with beaten egg yolk, roll in black noodles and set onto a lightly floured plate on the windowsill to dry.

Consommé
Meanwhile, make the consommé - season the reserved stock with salt, freshly ground pepper and the cinnamon. Bring to the boil, lower the heat and simmer for 2 minutes. Beat the egg whites in a bowl with the wine vinegar. Bring the stock back to the boil and add the egg whites, whisk once, and return to the slowest simmer. After 1 minute, cut a hole in the cooked egg whites. Simmer for a further 10-15 minutes, never boiling (see note below). Finally, strain through a sieve lined with muslin or cheesecloth into a clean pan. Keep hot.

To serve
Heat the oil to 180°C/350°F and deep-fry the gyoza until crisp. Drain on kitchen paper, on a cooling rack. Place two gyoza in each bowl, pour over the hot consommé and sprinkle with the finely chopped spring onions. Serve immediately.

Note
When making consommé the stock needs to be 'clarified' to make it beautifully clear. The egg white globules dispersed into the stock acts as a magnet for all the cloudy particles. These gradually rise to the surface, leaving a crystal-clear liquid below.

rabbit with beamish, prunes and spice

SERVES 4

2 large rabbits or 1 large robust chicken

STOCK

carcasses and bones from the rabbits
2 litres (3½ pints) approx. of water
1 onion, peeled and sliced
1 stick of celery, 1 carrot, sliced
a sprig each of thyme and parsley
6 peppercorns

BRAISING THE LEGS

legs and shoulders of the rabbits
flour to dredge
salt and freshly ground black pepper
50 g (2 oz) butter

575 ml (1 pint) of Beamish stout
1 litre (1¾ pints) stock from above
4 stars of anise
2 chillies, 4 cloves
20 peppercorns, 1 bay leaf
20 coriander seeds

2 leeks, sliced
2 sweet potatoes, diced
2 carrots, sliced
4 cloves of garlic, unpeeled
600 g (1lb 12oz) prunes pre-soaked

a small piece of roux, or 1 teaspoon of
arrowroot or cornstarch

Preparation
Joint the rabbits into legs, shoulders and loins. Remove the loins from the carcass and reserve. Chop the remaining carcass for the stock as small as possible.

Stock
Put all the ingredients into a large stockpot and pour in the water. Bring to the boil and skim the fat off the top with a metal spoon. Reduce the heat and simmer for 3-5 hours. Strain and remove any remaining fat. If you need a stronger flavour, boil down the liquid in an open pan to reduce by one third or half of the volume. Use as needed.

Braising the legs
Season the rabbit pieces with salt and freshly ground pepper and dredge lightly with flour.
Preheat the oven to 180°C/350°F/gas mark 4.
Heat 25g of the butter in a large oven proof casserole. Add the rabbit pieces and brown nicely on each side. Pour in the Beamish and the stock, stir well and cover with a lid. Bring the contents of the casserole to simmering point on top of the stove and transfer to the preheated oven. Simmer slowly for 30 minutes.
After 30 minutes remove from the oven and add the spices, the coarsely chopped vegetables and the prunes. Return to simmering point on top of the stove, transfer to the oven and braise for a further 30 minutes.
When the rabbit pieces are tender, remove the casserole from the oven, and strain the braising liquid through a fine sieve into a saucepan. Skim the surface fat off and discard. Thicken the braising liquid with a little roux, arrowroot or cornstarch to a consistency thick enough to coat a spoon nicely.
Taste and season with salt and freshly ground pepper. Return the sauce to the casserole and heat through over a gentle heat while you cook the loins.
Heat the remaining butter in a frying pan. Fry the loins until medium rare and remove to a heated plate. Carve into slices and keep warm.

To serve
Divide the braised meat and the loin slices between four warmed plates. Spoon a generous amount of the sauce and some prunes over this and serve.

rabbit with beamish, prunes and spice

"This dish is a variation of an often neglected classic of our habitat; here the underlying sweet and bitter tones of the rabbit are enhanced by the spices. Be careful that the 'heat' or chilli content remains suitably subdued by adding the chillies in the last stages, and tasting before adding more" Seamus O'Connell

crab and champ gratin,
with a tomato and chive dressing

SERVES 4

Preheat the oven to 200°C/400°F/gas mark 6.

CHAMP
4 potatoes
1 scallion finely chopped
25 g (1 oz) butter
salt and freshly ground
black pepper
pinch of nutmeg

Champ
Scrub the potatoes and cook them in boiling salted water in their jackets.
When cooked, peel and mash.
Sauté the scallions in the butter until soft (2-3 minutes).
Add the hot mashed potatoes, mix well and season with salt, pepper and grated nutmeg.
Divide the mixture between 4 buttered ramekins or 4 oven-proof bowls suitable for 1 serving.

CRAB MIXTURE
225 g (8 oz) white crab meat
275 ml (½ pint) fresh cream
juice and rind of half lemon
2 drops of tabasco sauce
salt and freshly ground
black pepper

Crab mixture
In a clean bowl, place the crab meat, cream, lemon juice and rind, tabasco, salt and pepper.
Mix thoroughly, taste and adjust seasoning.
Top up the four ramekins with this mixture and bake in the preheated oven for about 15 minutes until a golden crust forms on top.

DRESSING
90 ml (3 fluid oz) sunflower oil
1 teaspoon sugar
1 teaspoon Lakeshore wholegrain mustard,
Dijon or French mustard
60 ml (2 fluid oz) cider vinegar
(lemon juice or white wine vinegar
can be used instead)
salt and freshly ground
black pepper

1 tomato, skinned, de-seeded
and diced neatly
2 dessertspoons
finely chopped chives

Dressing
Put the oil, sugar, mustard and vinegar into a blender and run at medium speed for about a minute.
Put the chives and tomato into a small bowl and pour the dressing over this mixture.
Season to taste with salt and freshly ground pepper.

To serve
Place a hot crab and champ gratin in the centre of four warmed plates.
Spoon a few tablespoons of the tomato and chive dressing around and serve immediately with a little mixed salad on the side if you wish.

baked silver hake on crispy noodles,
with a bacon and thyme butter sauce

SERVES 4

4 x 175 g (6 oz) fish fillets
(John Dory, cod, turbot, brill, hake - for hake,
ask your fishmonger to scale the fish and
leave the skin on, and remove any bones)
lemon juice
salt and freshly ground pepper

SAUCE

5 tablespoons of dry white wine
2 tablespoons of white wine vinegar
1 teaspoon of finely chopped shallot
1 tablespoon of cream
70g (2¾ oz) of very cold diced butter
salt and freshly ground pepper

TO COOK THE FISH

25 g (1 oz) of butter

THE NOODLES

225 g (8 oz) noodles
pinch of salt
1 teaspoon of olive oil
25 g (1 oz) of butter
4 slices of streaky bacon
rind removed and finely chopped
1 sprig of fresh thyme
salt and freshly ground pepper

GARNISH

diced tomato concasse (optional)
4 sprigs of fennel

Drizzle some freshly squeezed lemon juice over the flesh side of the hake and season with salt and freshly ground pepper. Reserve.

Sauce
Put the vinegar, wine and shallot into a wide pan and boil over a high heat until the liquid has reduced to about two tablespoons. Add the cream, bring to the boil again, lower the heat and whisk in the butter, a small piece at a time.
Taste and season with salt and freshly ground pepper.
*Remember if you are using salted butter you may not need to add any salt at this point.
To keep the sauce warm, pour into a stainless steel jug and sit into a bowl of boiling water. Leave aside, stirring occasionally.

To cook the fish
Preheat the oven to 200°C/400°F/gas mark 6.
Melt the butter in a non-stick frying pan. When hot, but not smoking, fry the fish fillets, flesh side down until golden.
Transfer to a baking tray and again, placing the fillets flesh side down, cover with buttered greaseproof paper. Bake in the preheated oven for 5 minutes or until the fish becomes opaque right through.

To cook the noodles
Meanwhile, bring a large pot of water to the boil.
Toss in the noodles, add a pinch of salt and a teaspoon of olive oil and cook for 2-3 minutes. Stir the pot occasionally to separate the strands. When cooked, drain in a colander and refresh under cold running water. Melt the butter in a heavy based frying pan, and fry the finely chopped bacon until crisp. Remove from the heat and stir in the thyme leaves.
Remove half of the bacon and thyme mixture and add this to the reserved sauce. Add the noodles to the frying pan with the remaining bacon and thyme and toss over a high heat until they are crispy and golden. Taste and season with salt and freshly ground pepper.

To serve
Pour some of the sauce onto four warmed plates. Arrange the crispy noodles with the bacon and thyme in the centre of each plate and sit a fillet of silver hake, skin side up, on top. Garnish each plate with a little diced tomato or a sprig of fennel.

hot ice cream crackers with an orange coulis
orange and poppy seed ice cream, wrapped in filo pastry, shaped into a cracker and deep fried

SERVES 4

ICE CREAM
6 egg yolks
1 whole egg
2 tablespoons of white wine
1 measure of Cointreau
700 ml (1¼ pints) cream, whipped lightly
2 tablespoons of marmalade
2 tablespoons of poppy seeds
2 oranges, juice and rind

PASTRY
4 sheets of filo pastry
(available in most supermarkets)
30 g (1 oz) of butter, melted
sunflower oil for deep frying

ORANGE COULIS
the juice of 4 oranges and rind of 2
the juice of 1 lemon and
rind of half the lemon
1 cup of water
1¼ cups of sugar

GARNISH
a leaf of sweet geranium
or mint for each serving

Orange and poppy seed ice cream
Whisk yolks, egg and wine in a bowl until they form a ribbon in the mixture. When doing this, sit the bowl over a saucepan of boiling water but don't let the bowl touch the water or the egg mixture might curdle.
(This is made very easy if you have a portable Kenwood mixer, Braun Multi-Blender or similar.)
Put poppy seeds on a metal tray and toast under hot grill for thirty seconds. Melt marmalade with juice and rind of 2 oranges and allow to cool.
Add to the lightly whipped cream, with Cointreau and poppy seeds. Fold in gently.
Next fold this mixture into the egg mixture. Put into a freezer friendly container and freeze overnight.

Pastry
Spread four sheets of filo pastry on table. Brush lightly with the melted butter. Cut each sheet in half lengthways. Place a dessertspoon of frozen ice cream at the base of each half and roll up to the end. Scrunch each end together to look like a Christmas cracker. Put back in freezer until needed.
This part can be made a day in advance.

Sauce
Boil the rind of lemon and orange for 1 minute to remove bitterness, and strain. Next, bring the water and sugar to boil and simmer for approximately 3 minutes to soft ball stage (a drop placed in cold water should form a soft ball). Add the lemon juice and orange juice. Reduce to a sauce consistency. Add rind.

To test
Put a teaspoon of sauce onto an ice cold plate — sauce should be of pouring consistency. Leave to cool. This sauce will keep for two weeks in the refrigerator if stored in a sterilised jar.

To serve
Deep fry the filo pastry crackers in the sunflower oil and serve immediately on a pool of orange coulis with lightly whipped cream.
Garnish with a leaf of sweet geranium or mint.

hot ice cream crackers with an orange coulis

Since 1977 when the Lovett family first opened the doors
of their late Georgian house as a restaurant, they have
worked to maintain high standards, combining traditional
cuisine with innovative ideas.

strawberry tarts: page 44

grandma's christmas cake

300 g (10 oz) raisins
300 g (10 oz) sultanas
125 ml (4 fl oz) medium sherry
50 g (2 oz) walnuts, chopped
50 g (2 oz) almonds, ground
75 g (3 oz) glace cherries
75 g (3 oz) marmalade
250 g (½ lb) butter
250g (½ lb) dark muscavado sugar
250 g (½ lb) flour
3 eggs
250 g (½ lb) flour
pinch of salt
½ teaspoon mixed spice
½ teaspoon cinnamon

ALMOND ICING (MARZIPAN)
175 g (6 oz) icing sugar
175 g (6 oz) caster sugar
350 g (12 oz) ground almonds
1 egg
2 teaspoons of lemon juice
2 teaspoons whiskey or
Amaretto di Saronno (almond flavour liqueur)

GLAZE
2 tablespoons apricot jam
2 teaspoons water or lemon juice

ROYAL ICING
1 kg (2 lb) icing sugar
4 egg whites
2 teaspoon lemon juice
2 teaspoon glycerine

The ingredients listed will make about 4 lb of cake, filling an 20 cm (8 in) diameter cake tin.
It should be made 2-3 weeks before it is iced.

Preparation
Preheat the oven to 160°C/325°F/gas mark 3.
Line the cake tin with a double thickness of grease proof paper.
First, soak the raisins and sultanas in the sherry for 2-3 hours. Sift the flour with the salt and spices into a bowl, lifting the sieve up high to give the flour a good airing. Then divide mixture into three portions. Mix one portion with the prepared fruit, nuts and marmalade. Next in a separate large mixing bowl, whisk the butter and sugar together and continue beating until the mixture is very soft. Add the eggs one at a time, beating well between each one, then use a metal spoon to fold in the second portion of flour, using gentle folding movements and not beating (this will help to keep the air in the mix.) Now fold in the remaining flour, fruit, nuts and marmalade.

Turn the mixture into the prepared tin and smooth the top of the cake. Dip your fingers in warm water and moisten the surface very slightly. This will prevent the crust of the cake getting hard during the long cooking. Put the cake in the middle of the preheated oven and reduce the temperature to 140°C/275°F/gas mark 1. Bake for about 2½ hours, after which time you can test the cake by sticking a fine skewer in the centre. If it comes out quite clean the cake is done. Allow the cake to cool for about 30 minutes in the tin and then turn out onto a rack and leave until quite cold. Wrap the cake in cling film or grease proof paper and store in an airtight container. You can now feed it drink — port, brandy, rum or any nice liqueur until you need to ice it.

Marzipan
Sieve the icing sugar into a bowl. Add the caster sugar, ground almonds, egg, lemon juice and the preferred choice of drink. Mix together to a smooth dough. Do not handle the marzipan more than necessary otherwise it will become oily.

Applying marzipan

To help the marzipan to stick to the cake, brush the top surface with apricot glaze. Divide the paste by cutting off one third. Dust a working surface with icing sugar and roll the smaller piece of paste into an 20 cm (8 in) square. (Use the base of the tin as a guide.) Turn the cake upside down and place it centrally on the rolled out almond paste. Using a palette knife press the edges of the paste up all round the edges of the cake, then turn the cake the right way up.

Now dust the working surface again with icing sugar and roll out the rest of the paste, long enough to cover the sides. Divide this in half, brush the sides of the cake with apricot glaze and fix the two strips of almond past all around the sides. Seal the gaps between the marzipan on top and sides of the cake with a palette knife (warmed in hot water, then dried).

White Icing

White Royal Icing is the traditional covering for rich fruit cake. Sieve the icing sugar onto a plate. Beat the egg whites until frothy. Add the icing sugar a tablespoon at a time, beating well in between, until half the sugar has been used. Beat well for 5—10 minutes until the mixture grows in bulk and becomes fluffy.

Gradually add the lemon juice, glycerine and the remaining sugar, beating the mixture well after each addition. Keep beating until the icing stands in peaks and loses its shine.

Cover with a damp cloth and leave to stand for a couple of hours to let the air bubbles disperse.

Applying white icing

Spoon some icing onto the top of the cake, work the air bubbles out of the icing by spreading it vigorously to and fro across the top of the cake with a long palette knife. Take a ruler or palette knife in both hands, holding it at an angle of about 30 degrees to the top of the cake, and draw it towards you to level off the icing. Hold the ruler upright and run it around the side of the cake to scrape off any excess icing that has spread over the edges.

Rest the cake and cake board on top of a turntable or cake tin and using the palette knife, cover the sides with icing. Use a spatula or palette knife to smooth sides.

Leave the cake for at least 4 hours in a warm place to let the icing dry. Then you can apply a second thin layer of icing to give a smooth surface.

This cake can be decorated further with lettering and rough icing according to one's own taste.

Note: You can buy quite good roll-on icing from a kitchen shop. It looks good and is much more convenient if you don't have enough time to do it all yourself.

"The thing about Christmas cakes is that they take years to evolve. Firstly, they only get made once a year, so it is a year before you can correct the mistakes of the previous year. Secondly, they are best if you keep them for a couple of months, occasionally splashing a glass of port or brandy over them, by which time you have usually forgotten exactly how you made them in the first place. For this reason we eventually realised why it is Grandma who always knows best with Christmas cakes. So it is Grandma's recipe we now use. We have evolved it year after year, and now everyone seems to think it is just right."

strawberry tarts

SERVES 8

Pre-heat oven to 180°C/350°F/gas mark 4.

SHORTBREAD BASE
500 g (1 lb) flour
350 g (12 oz) butter
125 g (4 oz) caster sugar
1 tablespoon of water (optional)

FILLING FOR 500 G (1 LB) OF PASTRY
2 eggs
2 egg yolks
½ litre (18 fluid oz) milk
50 g (2 oz) sugar
30 g (1 oz) flour
31/2 g (½ oz) corn flour
1 vanilla pod
750 g (1½ lb) strawberries
per 500 g (1 lb) of pastry

GLAZE
3 tablespoons redcurrant jelly
1 dessertspoon of water

Shortbread pastry
Sift the flour into a large bowl, rub butter into flour as for shortcrust pastry, add the sugar and combine. A tablespoon of water may be necessary at this stage to work the ingredients to a smooth paste. Chill pastry in a refrigerator for 30 minutes. This will make 2 lb of pastry, half of which can be frozen for further use.
Proceed with 1 lb of pastry. Roll into shape for a 23 x 31 cm (9 x 121/2 in) buttered tin or alternatively, individual tartlet tins can be used. Line pastry with baking parchment, fill with baking beads, dried rice, or beans and bake blind in a moderate oven for 15-20 minutes.

Filling
Heat up milk with vanilla pod. Combine the eggs, yolks, sugar and flour in a separate saucepan. Pour hot milk onto egg mixture, slowly at first, whisking all the time. Stir over a very low heat until the custard is thick and cooked. Remove the vanilla pods.

Glaze
The glaze is an essential part of the taste and not just for decoration and you can use shop bought red currant jelly for this. Heat it up, hot but not boiling, stir in the dessertspoon of water.
Brush a little thinned red currant glaze onto the shortbread base, add the cream and arrange hulled (stalks removed) and halved strawberries.
Finally, carefully brush the glaze over the strawberries.

"It was a Christmas cake which really tripped us up in our first year in the Gingerbread House. Either the fruit sank, or else it floated to the top, or they were over-cooked or raw. But the worst bit was the icing. We made royal icing, but didn't know you had to put in a bit of glycerine or liquid glucose to make it a bit softer... as soon as we reopened again after Christmas, ladies started coming back with their cakes and stories of saws and axes. I had sent one to my parents, and they told me that even the pet Alsatian had given up on it. That year all our profits and more went on refunds for Christmas cakes." Barnaby Blacker

Issacs, Cork's busiest restaurant, is a bistro style informal eating place. Situated in a converted Victorian warehouse with high ceilings and brick walls, it is packed with atmosphere. The food served by chef Canice Sharkey is wide ranging in style and consistent in it's quality. All breads and icecreams are home made on the premises. Small wonder that reservations are advisable even on Sunday and Monday nights.

tagliatelle with asparagus, cream and parmesan

SERVES 4

225 g (8 oz) fresh Irish asparagus

PASTA
225 g (8 oz) tagliatelle
1 teaspoon of salt

TO ASSEMBLE
25 g (1 oz) butter
175 g (7 oz) cream
the reserved asparagus and pasta
50 g (2 oz) freshly grated parmesan
salt and freshly ground white pepper
pinch of nutmeg

The asparagus
To prepare the asparagus, hold the spear with its butt end up.
Peel off the skin and enough of the tough outer flesh to expose
the tender green portion underneath. Wash the peeled
asparagus spears in cold water and leave to drain.
Cook in boiling salted water for four to five minutes. Drain and
reserve.

Pasta
Cook the pasta by putting it into plenty of boiling salted water.
Simmer for approximately 12 minutes. It should be cooked
through but still al dente, i.e. with a bit of bite.

To serve
Melt the butter in a wide based pan and add half the cream.
Bring to the boil, reduce the heat and simmer for a couple of
minutes until the cream thickens slightly.
Add the asparagus, the hot drained tagliatelle, the remaining
cream and the Parmesan cheese. Season with salt, freshly
ground pepper and nutmeg. Toss briefly and adjust seasoning if
necessary. Serve immediately.

penne with red pepper sauce,
cream cheese and scallions

RED PEPPER SAUCE
1 tablespoon of olive oil
1 Spanish onion, peeled and finely chopped
4 firm red peppers, deseeded and chopped
2 cloves garlic peeled and crushed
½ fresh red chilli, finely chopped
salt and freshly ground black pepper
240 ml (8 fluid oz) fresh vegetable stock
240 ml (8 fluid oz) white wine
240 ml (8 fluid oz) cream

PASTA
350 g (12 oz) of penne
1 teaspoon of salt

TO SERVE
75-100 g (3-4 oz) cream cheese
8 scallions chopped
salt and freshly ground pepper
crusty white bread

Sauce
Heat the olive oil in a pan, add the onion and cook over a gentle heat for two to three minutes. Add the peppers, garlic, chilli, salt and freshly ground pepper, cover and sweat over a gentle heat for ten minutes.
Pour the vegetable stock and the white wine into the peppers, bring to the boil and reduce the liquid by half. Add the cream and stir well. Remove from the heat and liquidise until smooth, pass through a fine sieve and return to the pan. Season to taste with salt and freshly ground pepper.

Pasta
Cook the pasta in boiling salted water for approximately 12 minutes, or until just al dente, i.e. with a bit of bite. Drain in a colander.

To Serve
Reheat the sauce, adding first the scallions, the cream cheese, and finally the pasta. Check and adjust seasoning if necessary and serve immediately on warmed plates with crispy white bread.

penne with red pepper sauce,
cream cheese and scallions

grilled lamb steak with
caramelised shallots and champ

SERVES 4

4 lamb steaks each
weighing about 275 g (10 oz)

MARINADE
60 ml (2 fluid oz) extra virgin olive oil
juice of ½ lemon
2 cloves of garlic, crushed
salt and freshly ground
black pepper

CHAMP
900 g (2 lb) potatoes
50 g (2 oz) scallions, finely chopped
275 ml (½ pint) milk
50 g (2 oz) butter
salt and freshly ground black pepper

CARAMELISED SHALLOTS
450 g (1 lb) shallots, peeled
50 g (2 oz) butter
2 tablespoons of sugar
2 tablespoons of water
salt and freshly ground black pepper

SAUCE
120 ml (4 fluid oz) lamb stock
25 g (1 oz) cold diced butter
reserved cooking juices
salt and freshly ground black pepper

GARNISH
4 sprigs of flat leaf parsley or rosemary

Lamb steaks are usually cut horizontally across the leg. They can sometimes be a little tough so they take quite a bit of cooking and are best marinated for a few hours before cooking.

To marinate the lamb
Mix all the ingredients for the marinade in a large bowl. Add the lamb steaks and toss until they are well coated. Cover with cling film and leave to marinate for 2-3 hours.

Champ
Scrub the potatoes and cook them in boiling salted water in their jackets. Put the scallions and the cold milk into a saucepan and bring slowly to the boil. Adjust the heat and simmer gently for 3-4 minutes, then turn off the heat and leave to infuse. Peel and mash the potatoes while hot and mix in the boiling milk and scallions. Add the butter and beat until light and creamy. Season to taste with salt and freshly ground black pepper. Keep warm until needed.

Caramelised shallots
Melt the butter in a large sauté pan, and put in the shallots, closely packed together. Add a pinch of salt and freshly ground pepper, the sugar and the water. Cover and cook over a moderate heat for about 10 minutes. Remove the lid and cook for a further 5-10 minutes, stirring occasionally, until the liquid evaporates and the onions are melting and brown. Keep warm.

To cook the steaks
Pre-heat the oven to 200°C/400°F/gas mark 6.
Remove the lamb steaks from the marinade and dry them thoroughly.
Heat a grill pan until red hot and sear the steaks for three minutes on each side until they are nicely brown. Transfer to the preheated oven and continue cooking for approximately 8-10 minutes, depending on taste. Place the steaks on a plate and keep warm while you make the sauce.

Sauce
Remove the fat from the pan and de-glaze with the lamb stock.
Bring to the boil and simmer for a few minutes until the stock is reduced by two thirds. Whisking gently, add the diced butter a little at a time, until the sauce thickens to a light coating consistency. Taste, and adjust seasoning if necessary.

To serve
Put two tablespoons of champ in the centre of four warmed deep plates and arrange six shallots in a circle surrounding it.
Cut each lamb steak in half and place on top of the champ. Spoon the sauce over the meat and garnish with a sprig of flat leaf parsley or rosemary.

marinated wild mushrooms with asparagus
on fresh linguini and pesto

SERVES 4

MARINADE

100 g (4 oz) mixed wild mushrooms
(chanterelles, trompets and
oyster mushrooms)

100 ml (3 fluid oz) white wine vinegar

2 whole cloves of garlic

5 sprigs of thyme

2 bay leaves

ASPARAGUS AND TOMATO

12 asparagus spears

4 tomatoes

LINGUINI

120 g (4 oz) fresh linguini

100 g (4 oz) pesto

FOR COOKING THE MUSHROOMS

15 ml (½ fluid oz) olive oil

15 ml (½ fluid oz) balsamic vinegar

GARNISH

4 sprigs of dill

Preparing the marinade

Trim the dried section of the stalk off the mushrooms. Wash them briefly and pat dry. Blanch in boiling salted water for 10 seconds. Drain in a colander and pat dry again.

Put the white wine vinegar, the whole garlic cloves, thyme and bay leaves into a bowl and mix well.

Add the mushrooms and leave to marinate for 24 hours.

Asparagus

To prepare the asparagus, hold the spear with its butt end up. Peel off the skin and enough of the tough outer flesh to expose the tender green portion underneath. Wash the peeled asparagus spears.

Bring a large saucepan of salted water to the boil. Cook the asparagus spears for 3-4 minutes. Drain and refresh under cold running water.

Tomatoes

Next, blanch the tomatoes for 8 seconds, drain and refresh. Peel, de-seed and chop the tomatoes into dice, or concassé.

Cooking the mushrooms

Heat the olive oil in a frying pan, remove the mushrooms from the marinade and cook briefly over a high heat, stirring all the time. Pour over the marinade liquid, and add the balsamic vinegar. Continue to cook over a high heat until they are cooked through. Season to taste with salt and freshly ground black pepper. Keep warm.

Linguini
Cook the linguini in plenty of boiling salted water for
approximately 3 minutes.
Drain and toss with the pesto until it is well coated.
Season to taste

To serve
Heat the asparagus briefly in boiling salted water.
Make four twists of the linguini with a fork and place in
the centre of four warmed plates.
Divide each plate into 3 sections with the warm asparagus
and spoon equal amounts of the mushrooms and sauce
into each section.
Sprinkle the tomato concasse around the linguini and
decorate with a sprig of dill.

Built in a Neo-Georgian style in 1995 and set in 2 acres of beautiful mature

gardens, Hayfield House is located in what were formerly the orchards of the

original Hayfield House.

roast loin of venison
with saffron risotto, spinach and red wine sauce

SERVES 4

750 g (1¾ lb) venison loin

RISOTTO

200 g (7 oz) arborio rice
(risotto rice)
½ onion finely chopped
1 litre (1¾ pints) chicken stock
200 ml (7 fluid oz) white wine
2g (pinch) saffron
50 g (2 oz) parmesan cheese grated
50 g (2 oz) butter

SPINACH

20 g (¾ oz) butter
2 shallots finely chopped
½ clove of garlic crushed
500 g (1 lb 2 oz) spinach
salt and freshly ground black pepper
pinch of nutmeg

RED WINE SAUCE

1 small onion finely chopped
1 stalk of celery chopped
5 cloves of garlic crushed
1 small red bell pepper chopped
1 tablespoon of olive oil
2 small tomatoes
skinned, de-seeded and chopped
120 ml (4 fluid oz) balsamic vinegar
2 tablespoons of port wine
1 bottle of red wine
(Cabernet Sauvignon or Zinfandel)

GARNISH

4 sprigs of chervil or parsley

Preheat the oven to 180°C/350°F/gas mark 4.

Preparing the venison
Trim all sinew and fat off the loin and tie with string. Season with salt and freshly ground pepper. Heat an oven proof pan over a moderate heat, add some oil, then seal the loin on all sides and place in the preheated oven for 7-9 minutes. Remove from the pan and rest for a few minutes. Cut off the string.

Risotto
Melt the butter in a large pan over a moderate heat. Add the onions and fry them gently until they are soft but not coloured. Stir in the rice and allow it to cook with the onions for 2 minutes, stirring well. Add the wine and the saffron and cook for a few minutes, stirring continuously. Pour in enough boiling stock to barely cover the rice. Stir gently until the stock has been absorbed, then add another ladleful of stock and continue in this way for about 20 minutes until the rice is just cooked. There should be enough liquid to give the risotto a creamy texture. Stir in the parmesan cheese and season to taste with salt and freshly ground pepper.

Spinach
Remove the stems from the spinach and wash twice in clean cold water. Drain in a colander and pat dry with a towel. Melt the butter in a pan and add the shallots and garlic. Cook for a few seconds and then add the spinach. Season with salt and pepper. Cover and cook at full boil for 2 minutes. Remove the lid, stir and cook for a further minute. Taste, correct seasoning, and add the nutmeg.

Red wine sauce
Heat the olive oil in a heavy based pan. Add the onions, celery, garlic and red pepper. Cover and sweat over a gentle heat for 8-10 minutes. Add the tomatoes, balsamic vinegar and port and reduce to a glaze. Pour in the wine, bring to the boil again and reduce until there is about 150 ml (5 fluid oz) of liquid left. Using a spoon skim off any fat and residue from the surface. Strain through cheesecloth into a clean saucepan. Taste and adjust seasoning if necessary.

roast loin of venison with saffron risotto, spinach and red wine sauce

To serve
Divide the spinach into four portions and place as a bed
on warmed plates. Mould the risotto into rings in the
centre. Reheat the venison and carve into 16 equal sized
pieces. Place four slices on each plate around the risotto.
Pour over a little sauce and then garnish with fresh
herbs such as chervil or parsley.

noix de st. jacques
scallops with parmesan discs and champagne sauce

SERVES 4

Scallops are at their best during the months from October to February.

SAUCE
520 g (1 lb 3 oz) of mixed root vegetables (onion, carrot, leek, celery)
600 ml (1 pint) of fish stock
3 bay leaves
50 g (2 oz) of tarragon
275 ml (½ pint) of champagne (or sparkling wine)
600 ml (1 pint) single cream
salt and freshly ground white pepper

PARMESAN DISCS
200 g (7 oz) fresh parmesan, finely grated (Parmigiano Reggiano)

Sauce
Wash and peel equal quantities of the mixed root vegetables.
Divide them in half and place on two separate plates. Finely chop one half of the vegetables and sweat them over a gentle heat until soft but not coloured. Reserve the second batch.
Add the fish stock, the bay leaf, and the tarragon, bring to the boil and reduce by two thirds. Pour in the champagne and boil again to reduce by two thirds. Finally, add the cream, bring to the boil, lower the heat and simmer gently until the sauce reduces to a consistency thick enough to coat the back of a spoon. Season to taste with salt and freshly ground white pepper.
Strain through a fine sieve into a clean pan and reserve.

Parmesan discs
Preheat the oven to 180°C/350°F/gas mark 4.
Draw out 8 circles with a 15 cm (6 in) diameter on a sheet of parchment paper or Bakewell and place these on a baking tray.
Carefully fill each of the marked out shapes with a tablespoon of grated parmesan. Spread the cheese in an even layer to the edges of the circles.
Bake in the preheated oven for 2-3 minutes until the cheese discs are melted and lightly browned. Remove from the oven and allow to cool on the tray. You can perfect the shape with a round cutter before they become cold.

SCALLOPS

12 scallops

25 g (1 oz) of butter

the reserved root vegetables

salt and freshly ground pepper

GARNISH

4 sprigs of either fennel,

dill or deep fried basil

Scallops

Detach the corals from the scallops, remove the white ligament from the side of each scallop meat and discard. Wash well and leave to dry on kitchen paper. Cut the remaining vegetables into small matchstick strips about 2.5 cm (1 in) long.

Melt 25 g (1 oz) of butter in a large frying pan. Season the scallops with salt and freshly ground pepper and as soon as the butter starts to foam add the scallops and cook briefly for about 30 seconds on each side, turning only once. Remove from the pan and keep warm.

In the same pan fry the vegetable strips over a high heat for about 4 minutes, until they are barely tender. Reserve.

To serve

Reheat the champagne sauce.

Place a parmesan disc in the centre of four warmed plates. Arrange three scallops on top of each disc and spoon over a little of the sauce. Top with another parmesan disc and garnish with a herb of your choice.

tarte au citron

SERVES 8

Preheat oven to 200°C/400°F/gas mark 6.

SWEET PASTRY
500 g (1 lb) flour
250 g (8 oz) butter
125 g (4 oz) sugar
1 egg

FILLING
juice of 5 lemons
zest of 2 lemons
450 g (14 oz) of caster sugar
275 g (9 fluid oz) of double cream
9 medium eggs

Pastry
Firstly make sure all your utensils are very cold.
Cut butter into cubes, add the flour and with fingertips
rub to a light fine crumb texture. Make a well in the
centre and add the beaten egg and sugar. Blend with
sufficient water until pastry is bound together in a nice
round shape. Leave for 45 minutes in the refrigerator.
Remove from the refrigerator and roll to fit a 30 cm (12
in) buttered flan ring.
Bake blind in the oven for 15 minutes, remove and
allow to cool.
Note: To bake blind put baking parchment in the centre
of the pastry with dried rice, beans, or baking beads.

Filling
Squeeze the lemons. Beat the eggs and sugar together,
add in the lemon juice and zest and whisk. Carefully
fold in the double cream until all the ingredients are
fully incorporated.
Pour the filling onto the pastry case. Bake in the oven at
150°C (300°F) for a further 30 minutes.
Remove from oven and allow to cool.

To serve
Top with dusted icing sugar.

"My very first experience of tasting the culinary delight of French cuisine was a mouth-watering bite of Tarte Au Citron. It was while on holiday at a little known village in France called Montingnac Le Coq. Having been reared on a diet of desserts which consisted of the traditional puddings and pies, it was a totally new experience. Still in my first decade of life and feeling very much a big man on my first holiday abroad, I sat mesmerised at the French making a hames of bowling. I threw my hat at it and proceeded to sample the remains of a good Monbazillac which some unobservant adults left lying around in a half empty glass, followed by gigantum portions of tarte au citron. Was it the wine? Was it the tart?" (Michael Fleming)

cod dijon

SERVES 4

4 x 225 g (8 oz) fillets of cod
(plaice or hake can also be used)

MUSTARD TOPPING
1 tablespoon of grainy Dijon mustard
2 tablespoons of smooth Dijon mustard
1 tablespoon of honey

TOMATO SALSA
225 g (8 oz) fresh red tomatoes,
skinned and de-seeded
40 g (1½ oz) scallions, finely chopped
1 teaspoon of toasted black mustard seeds
2 tablespoons of French dressing
salt and freshly ground pepper
½ red chilli, finely chopped (optional)

GARLIC CRUMBS
125 g (4 oz) fresh white bread crumbs
1 clove of garlic, crushed
1 tablespoon of olive oil
1 tablespoon of parsley, finely chopped

Preheat the oven to 200°C/400°F/gas mark 6.

Mustard topping
Combine both mustards and the honey together in a
bowl and mix to a smooth paste.

Tomato salsa
Cut the tomato into dice and place in a bowl with all the
other ingredients, season to taste with salt and freshly
ground pepper and mix well.

Garlic crumbs
Put the bread crumbs into a small bowl.
Stir in the crushed garlic, the olive oil and the parsley
and mix well. Season to taste with salt and freshly
ground black pepper.

Preparation and cooking
Place the cod fillets, skin side down, on a lightly oiled
baking tray. Spread the mustard topping evenly over the
flesh side of the fish. Bake in the preheated oven for 5
minutes.
Remove from the oven and cover the fish with the
tomato salsa. Return to the oven and continue cooking
for a further 2 minutes.
Finally, remove the fish from the oven again and top
with the garlic crumbs. Bake for another 3 minutes
(approximately) until the crumbs are lightly brown.

Serving suggestion
This cod dish can be served on a bed of potato
surrounded with stir fried greens.
See overleaf for several potato options!

stir fried greens

4 florets of broccoli
1 medium courgette
4 scallions
16 mangetout
a handful of spinach
1 tablespoon of olive oil
1 tablespoon of sesame seed oil
salt and freshly ground pepper
1 tablespoon of sesame seeds

Preparing the vegetables
Blanch the broccoli by dropping it into boiling salted water. Bring it back to the boil, remove the florets immediately with a slotted spoon and refresh in cold water.
Trim the scallions, leave the white section long and shred the green section.
Cut the courgettes in half lengthways and slice them at an angle.
Trim the mangetout and leave them whole.
Shred the spinach leaves finely.

To cook
Heat 1 tablespoon of olive oil in a wok or deep frying pan until it smokes. Add the white section of the scallions and toss. Add the courgettes and the mangetout and stir fry for 1 minute. Add the spinach and the scallion greens and stir fry for 1 minute further.
Finally, add the sesame seeds and the sesame seed oil and season with salt and freshly ground pepper. Toss well until all the vegetables are heated through. Remove to a hot serving dish and serve immediately.

"17 years on. . . and nothing stays the same, except for the ever growing selection of good produce we have to choose from which makes for continuous excitement. We are indebted to our suppliers for our continuous supply of fresh fish, our locally reared ducks, our good beef and lamb and 'organic Jo' for our wonderful and ever increasing variety of organic vegetables. The recipes we have chosen can be used in many different ways. We hope you enjoy the flavours, and happy cooking." Jacqui Barry

three recipes for potato

BASIC RECIPE
1 kg (22 lb) 'old' potatoes, e.g.
Kerr's Pinks or Golden Wonder

Scrub the potatoes and leave them in their jackets. Put them into a saucepan of cold water, add a good pinch of salt and bring to the boil. When the potatoes are half cooked (about 15 minutes) strain off most of the water and replace the lid on the saucepan. Reduce the heat to very low and allow the potatoes to steam until they are cooked. Peel and mash the potatoes while hot.
Use as the basis for recipe options (1), (2) or (3) below.

(1) CHAMP
2 bunches of scallions, finely chopped
80 ml (22 fluid oz) fresh cream
75 g (3 oz) butter
salt and freshly ground pepper

(1) Champ
Cover the scallions with cold milk and bring slowly to the boil. Lower the heat and simmer for 3-4 minutes, then turn off the heat and leave to infuse.
Mix the boiling milk and scallions into the hot mashed potatoes and add the butter. Beat until light and creamy and season to taste with salt and freshly ground pepper.

(2) OLIVE OIL MASH
80 ml (22 fluid oz) extra virgin olive oil
2 tablespoons of freshly chopped parsley
salt and freshly ground pepper

(2) Olive Oil Mash
Heat the olive oil in a small saucepan. Add to the hot mashed potatoes and beat until light and fluffy.
Season to taste with salt and freshly ground pepper and mix in the freshly chopped parsley.

(3) COLCANNON
450 g (1 lb) cooked cabbage
(equal to 2 heads of green
spring cabbage raw)
250 ml (8 fluid oz) milk
2 scallions, finely chopped
75 g (3 oz) butter
salt and freshly ground pepper

(3) Colcannon
Remove the dark outer leaves from the cabbage. Wash and cut into quarters, remove the core and cut finely across the grain. Cook in a small amount of boiling salted water until tender. Drain, season with salt and freshly ground pepper.
Cover the scallions with cold milk and bring slowly to the boil, reduce the heat and simmer for 3-4 minutes. Turn off the heat and leave to infuse.
Mix the boiling milk and scallions into the hot mashed potatoes, add the butter and beat until you have a fluffy purée. Stir in the cooked cabbage and season to taste with salt and freshly ground pepper.

pan grilled fish
with flavoured butters

SERVES 4

4 x 175 g (6 oz) of
very fresh fish fillets
seasoned flour
a knob of softened butter

MUSTARD BUTTER
125 g (4 oz) softened butter
1 tablespoon of
smooth Dijon mustard
1 tablespoon of
grainy Dijon mustard

ANCHOVY BUTTER
125 g (4 oz) softened butter
50 g (2 oz) anchovies

TOMATO VINAIGRETTE
Makes 300 ml (½ pint)
1 clove of garlic
½ teaspoon of granulated sugar
2 large ripe red tomatoes,
skinned and de-seeded
2 tablespoons of white wine vinegar
150 ml (5 fluid oz) olive oil
75 ml (2½ fluid oz) vegetable oil
salt and freshly ground pepper

The following flavoured butters can be served with cod or almost any fish which has been pan grilled, grilled or baked.

Heat the grill, pan grill or preheat the oven to 200°C/400°F/gas mark 6.
Dip the fish fillets in well seasoned flour. Shake off the excess and, using a knife, spread a little softened butter as thinly as possible over the flesh side of the fillets.
If you are using the grill or oven, place the fish fillets, flesh side up, and cook for 10-15 minutes approximately, depending on the thickness of the fish.
If, however, you are using a pan grill, heat until quite hot, place the fillets butter side down, and cook for 4-5 minutes on that side. Turn over and cook on the other side until crisp and golden.
Serve the fish on hot plates with a few slices of any of the following flavoured butters.

Mustard butter
Beat the butter until light and creamy, add both mustards and mix well. Either put into a bowl in the refrigerator or form into a roll and refrigerate until needed.
This butter could also be spread on the flesh side of the fish fillet before baking or grilling.

Anchovy butter
Put the anchovies and the butter together in a food processor and process until well blended. As before, form into a roll and refrigerate until needed.

Tomato Vinaigrette
This is a very versatile recipe which can be mixed through tagliatelle to accompany any white fish. It can also be used with chicken or in a salad.
Put the garlic into a blender and crush to a paste.
Add the sugar, the tomatoes and the wine vinegar, and blend until you achieve a fairly smooth texture.
Adjust the speed setting to slow and gradually add the oils, separately, until well emulsified. The vinaigrette should be smooth.
Finally, season to taste with salt and freshly ground pepper.

peach melba
baked peaches in red wine, mascarpone cream
and iced strawberry mousse

SERVES 4

ICED STRAWBERRY MOUSSE
225 g (8 oz) of strawberries
juice of ½ lemon
90 g (3 oz) caster sugar
I egg white

PEACHES
4 peaches peeled and stoned
glass of red wine
2 vanilla pods
2 cinnamon sticks
juice and rind of ½ lemon
110 g (4 oz) caster sugar

MASCARPONE CREAM
60 g (2 oz) mascarpone cheese
400 g (14 oz) carton of cream

Preheat the oven to 180°C/325°F/gas mark 3.

Mousse
This needs to be made the previous day to give it time
to freeze. Raspberries can be substituted for
strawberries.
Whisk egg white and sugar until stiff.
Pulp strawberries in a blender.
Add strawberries and lemon juice to egg mixture. Whisk
for a further 20 minutes until it has trebled in volume.
Taste and freeze.

Peaches
Halve the peaches, skin and stone.
In a heavy pan put the red wine, vanilla pod, cinnamon
stick, lemon juice and rind, and caster sugar.
Add the 4 halved peaches to the red wine mixture.
Cover with grease proof paper and bake gently in oven
for 25-30 minutes. When soft, remove the peaches and
reduce liquid by half and strain. This liquid can be used
as the coulis.

Mascarpone cream
Whisk the cream until fluffy. Gently blend in cheese.

To serve
Place each peach on a plate, scoop out the frozen
mousse into balls and place on top of the peaches.
Dribble coulis on top, and decorate with some
strawberries.

peach melba. baked peaches in red wine, mascarpone cream and iced strawberry mousse

ragout of scallops and prawns
with prune infusion

SERVES 4

Scallops, prawns and shrimps are at their best from the months of October to February.

4 prunes
12 fresh prawns
8 large fresh sea scallops
2 shallots, peeled
1 bunch of fresh chervil

100 ml (3½ fluid oz) olive oil
salt and freshly ground pepper
150 ml (5 fluid oz) Noilly Prat
(French Vermouth)
100 ml (3 fluid oz) prune juice
260 ml (9 fluid oz) fresh cream

GARNISH
25 g (1 oz) approx.
fresh rocket leaves

Preparation
Soak the prunes in warm water for 45 minutes. Remove and reserve the juice. Chop into very fine dice and set aside.
Peel and devein the prawns, wash well and pat dry with kitchen paper.
Detach the corals from the scallops, remove the white ligament from the side of each scallop meat and discard. Wash well and leave to dry on kitchen paper.
Finely dice the shallots.
Wash and dry the chervil, and chop finely.
Wash and dry the rocket leaves and arrange into 4 small bouquets for the garnish.

To cook
Heat the oil in a large sauté pan until very hot. Cut the scallops in half lengthways, and season with salt and freshly ground pepper. Lay them in a single layer on the pan and sauté until lightly browned, turning only once.
Add the prawns and chopped shallots and stir gently until they begin to colour lightly.
Pour in the Noilly Prat, bring to the boil and reduce by half.
Add the prune juice and boil again to reduce by half.
Remove the scallops and prawns to a warmed plate with a slotted spoon and keep warm.
Finally, pour in the cream, bring to the boil and reduce by half. Lower the heat and add the finely chopped prunes, the chopped chervil, the scallops and the prawns.
Simmer gently until everything is heated through. Taste, and adjust seasoning if necessary.

To serve
Divide the ragout between four warmed plates and garnish with the bouquet of rocket leaves.

ragout of scallops and prawns with prune infusion

Bought in 1961 by the Ryan family, the Arbutus Lodge stands in its own gardens
overlooking the city of Cork. Run as a small family hotel with an excellent restaurant,
it enjoys a local and international reputation. Their tasting menu features seven
courses of the specialities of the day.

loin of lamb roasted and glazed with honey,
mustard and baked shallots in sea salt with balsamic syrup

SERVES 4

2 loin of lamb total weight
approx. 675 g (24 oz)

GLAZE
100 ml (3 fluid oz) clear honey
150 ml (5 fluid oz) Dijon mustard
2 teaspoons of finely chopped
fresh rosemary

SHALLOTS
12 large shallots, unpeeled
500 g (18 oz) coarse sea salt

TO COOK
1 tablespoon of olive oil
salt and freshly ground pepper
125 g (4 oz) approx. white
bread crumbs

SYRUP
260 ml (9 fluid oz) balsamic vinegar
100 ml (3 fluid oz) approx.
extra virgin olive oil

GARNISH
4 sprigs of flat leaf parsley

Preparation

Preheat the oven to 200°C/400°F/gas mark 6.

Trim all sinew and fat off the loins and season with salt and freshly ground black pepper.

Mix the honey, mustard and rosemary together to make a paste.

Place the shallots in a single layer on a baking tray and cover with the sea salt.

To cook

Place the shallots in the hot oven and bake for 20 minutes.

Meanwhile, heat the olive oil in a sauté pan over a moderate heat and sear the loins on all sides for 1 minute until lightly coloured, remove to a baking tray. Adjust the oven temperature to 190°C/375°F/gas mark 5. Brush the lamb with the honey and mustard glaze and cover completely with the bread crumbs.

Roast in the oven for 15 minutes, remove and leave to rest on a warm plate, loosely covered with foil.

Remove the shallots from the oven, peel off the skins and discard along with the salt. Place on a heated plate and keep warm.

Syrup

Put the balsamic vinegar in a stainless steel saucepan, bring to the boil and reduce by two-thirds. Remove from the heat and allow to cool.

To serve

Drizzle a thin line of olive oil around the outer edge of four warmed plates and using a teaspoon, allow a little of the balsamic syrup to run off the spoon onto the olive oil.

Carve the lamb into 16 equal sized slices and arrange four of these in the centre of each plate, with edges overlapping. Surround with 3 shallots and garnish with the sprigs of flat leaf parsley.

strawberries au gratin
flavoured with baileys

SERVES 4

625g (1¼ lb) strawberries
150ml (3 fl oz) Baileys
4 large egg yolks
50g (2 oz) caster sugar
400ml (15 fl oz) cream
mint to garnish

Wash and dry strawberries. Remove stalks and cut in half. Arrange strawberries in a high sided heat resistant dish or bowl.

In a separate bowl, combine the egg yolks, sugar and Baileys and place over a pot of boiling water. Whisk quickly until the mixture becomes thick and creamy. Remove from the boiling water and allow to cool slightly.

Whisk the cream into soft peaks and gently fold into the egg mixture to form a sabayon. Cover strawberries with the sabayon and brown under a grill or with a blow torch. Garnish with a little picked mint and serve.

bouffe du roi

"I learned this from an old docker at Port St. Louis on the Bouche du Rhône near Marseilles. He was trying to teach me the noble value of simple peasant fare.
On the way to his cabanon, built on a sand spit on the right bank of the Rhône with the Camargue swamps stretching to the west, I steered the boat with my foot while stirring a wooden spoon to act as Kenwood for Fernand's aïoli.
In the cabanon we lit a driftwood fire to grill some saucisson but it was the hors d'oeuvre which took my fancy; Bouffe du Roi, Fernand called it.
There is no preparation or cooking involved apart from sourcing the ingredients.
It may not sound appetising and it isn't always a suitable starter, but many of our friends are now hooked, even some who didn't like anchovies."

SERVES 4

1-2 tins of anchovy fillets in olive oil
extra virgin olive oil
good white bread such as,
ciabatta, foccacia or baguette
8 spring onions or shallots

TO SERVE

a bottle of well chilled
dry rosé or white vin ordinaire

Prepare enough of all the ingredients to satisfy 4 people and place in the centre of the table.
Each person can help themselves in the following way.

Make a puddle on your plate with the oil from the anchovies mixed with a little extra virgin olive oil. Soak up some oil with a small chunk of bread and add to this one or two anchovy fillets and a generous chunk of onion.
Every mouthful needs to have plenty of everything in it.

To serve
Wash down with a nice glass of wine.

the iago food company in the english market, Cork

Iago is a stall in the English market specialising in Irish and European farmhouse cheeses as well as Spanish and Italian products. Proprietor Sean Calder-Potts has created a unique atmosphere where you can watch pasta being made and subsequently taste it freshly cooked. Clientele stand at the counter in the midst of the busy bustle of fish-selling across the way.

72

73

tripe and drisheen
from the english market

SERVES 2

450 g (1 lb) honeycomb tripe
225 g (½ lb) drisheen
1 litre (1¾ pints) milk approx.
1 large onion peeled and thinly sliced
3 teaspoons of Dijon mustard
2 sprigs of fresh thyme
salt and freshly ground pepper to taste

Preparation
Soak the tripe for several hours or overnight in several changes of cold water. Remove, and wash thoroughly under cold, running water. Cut the tripe into 5 cm (2 in) pieces and place in a heated dry saucepan.
Soak the drisheen in cold water for 10 minutes. Remove the skin and cut into similar sized pieces as the tripe.

To Cook
In an open pan, sweat the tripe over a gentle heat for approximately 1 hour. Add a little milk occasionally, to prevent the tripe drying out.
Add the onion, mustard, thyme, salt and pepper and the remaining milk and continue to simmer for a further half hour.
When the tripe is cooked, thicken the sauce with a little roux (equal quantities of butter and flour cooked together for 2 minutes over a gentle heat).

Add the drisheen to the tripe and onion mixture and heat through gently, stirring constantly. Adjust seasoning if necessary and serve with crusty bread and boiled floury potatoes (in good Cork tradition, skin and all).

Farmgate Café at the English Market

There are two Farmgate Restaurants. The first, established in 1984 by Máróg O'Brien in Midleton, started as a specialised food shop and now combines this with a large restaurant. An extensive range of breads and cakes are freshly produced in the pattisserie and these are also supplied to the Cork City Farmgate Restaurant and Café which has a dramatic location in the English Market. The second restaurant, run by Máróg and Kay Harte has been in operation since 1994 when the two discovered that the English market had an upstairs.

"I took myself up 'those steps', steps I had never even noticed being there before - lo and behold, there it was, another challenge." Máróg O'Brien

farmgate queen of puddings

SERVES 6-8

Preheat the oven to 190°C/375°F/gas mark 5.

PUDDING
568 ml (1 pint) milk or more
568 ml (1 pint) cream
1 vanilla pod
7 egg yolks
75 g (3 oz) caster sugar
500 g (1 lb) soft white breadcrumbs
6 tablespoons of strawberry jam

Pudding
Combine the milk, cream and vanilla pod and bring to
the boil. Remove from the heat.
Whisk the egg yolks and 75 g (3 oz) of caster sugar and
add to the liquid. Stir in the breadcrumbs and then
empty into a buttered oval pyrex (ovenproof) dish. Cook
until set, for approximately 40 minutes.
When the base of the pudding has cooled, spread with
the strawberry jam.

MERINGUE
7 egg yolks
175 g (6 oz) caster sugar

Adjust the oven temperature to 200°C/400°F/gas mark 6.

Meringue
Meanwhile whisk the egg whites. Add half the caster
sugar and beat until stiff, and then fold in the remaining
caster sugar.
Top with the meringue mixture, return to the oven and
bake until nicely browned.

To Serve
Serve with a little lightly whipped unsweetened cream.

"The Farmgate is about no compromise regarding materials. The produce is high-quality, 'under handled', and is light, fresh and simply executed."

Máróg O'Brien

cork

county

pan fried cod with puy lentils and green salsa

pan fried cod
with puy lentils and green salsa

SERVES 4

LENTILS
225 g (8 oz) puy lentils
juice of 1 lemon
575 ml (1 pint) chicken stock
1 small onion, stuck with 2 cloves
1 bay leaf
salt and freshly ground black pepper

GREEN SALSA
8-10 mint and basil leaves
1 bunch of flat leaf parsley
2 cloves garlic, roughly chopped
1 tablespoon Dijon mustard
1 dessertspoon capers
4 anchovies
150 ml (¼ pint) extra virgin olive oil
salt and freshly ground
black pepper to taste

TO COOK THE FISH
1 tablespoon of olive oil
4 x 175 g (6 oz) fillets of cod
salt and freshly ground pepper

GARNISH
4 lemon wedges

In this recipe you can pan grill, poach or oven-bake the fish, as you prefer.

Cooking the lentils
Wash the lentils and put into a stainless steel saucepan. Add the lemon juice, chicken stock, onion and bay leaf. Bring slowly to the boil, reduce the heat and simmer for 30-40 minutes until the lentils are cooked and the stock absorbed.
Remove and discard the onion and bay leaf and season to taste while still warm.

Salsa
Put all the ingredients for the salsa in a liquidiser. Add a few drops of olive oil and process in an on/off method until the mixture is finely chopped. Slowly add the remaining oil, and season to taste with salt and freshly ground pepper.

Cooking the fish
Preheat the oven to 230°C/450°F/gas mark 8.
Score the fish quite deeply to prevent it from curling.
Brush the fillets with a light film of olive oil and season with salt and freshly ground pepper. Heat a pan grill until quite hot and place the fillets, skin side down in the pan.
Cook until a nice crust forms. Turn the fillets over and finish cooking, skin side up in the preheated oven.

To serve
Divide the lentils between four warmed plates and arrange a cod fillet, skin side up, on top of the lentils.
Garnish with a wedge of lemon and serve the green salsa on the side.

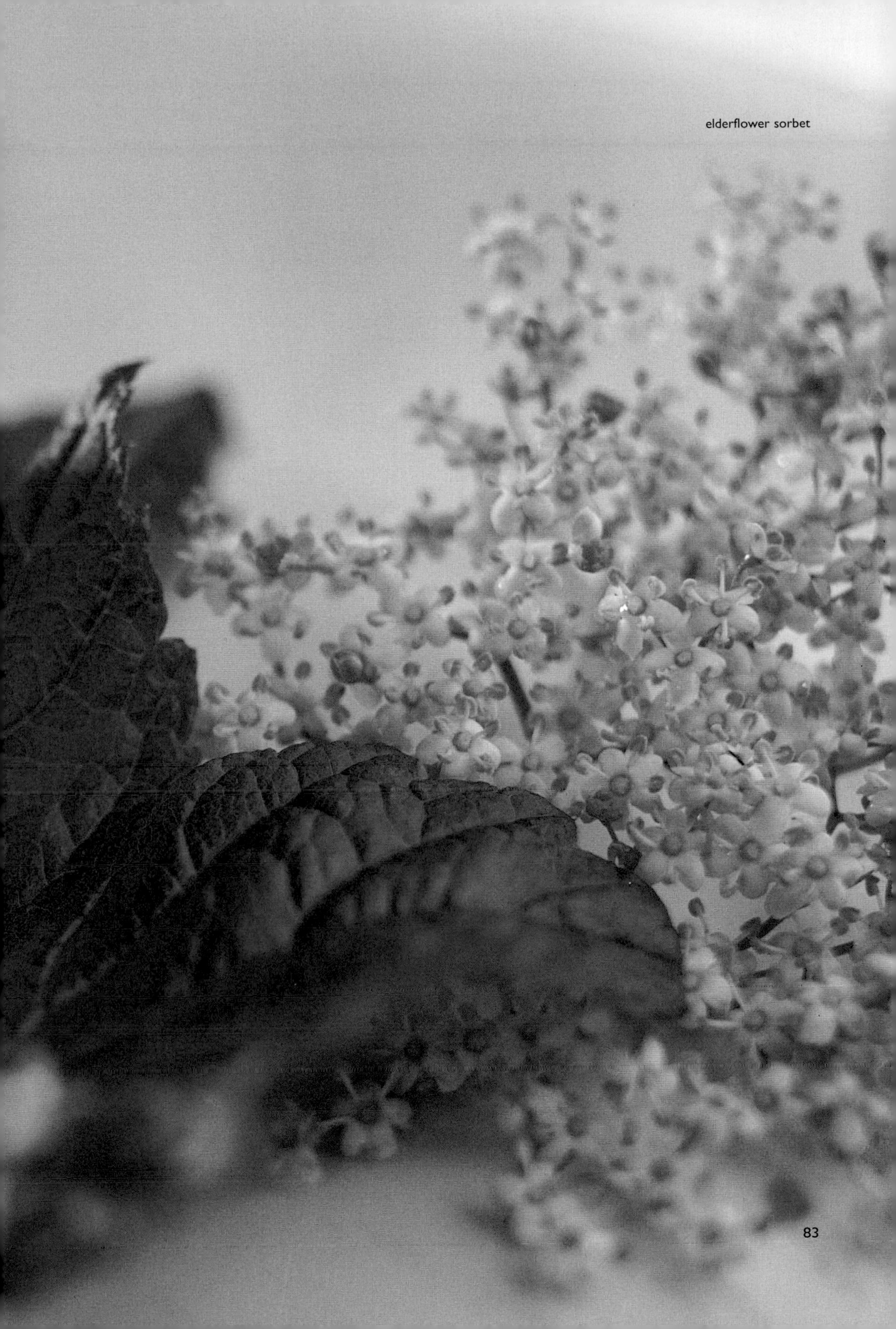
elderflower sorbet

nettle soup

Nettles made an appearance almost six thousand years ago when the first farmers cut down forest trees to clear the ground for crop cultivation, and were commonly used to make soup and pottage. The nettle soup is said to have been a favourite of St. Colmcille. Nettles were also used as a vegetable in famine times.

SERVES 6-8

250 g (½ lb) organic nettle tops
175 g (6 oz) butter
4 cloves of garlic
500 g (1 lb) onions
1.7 litres (3 pints) water
1 heaped teaspoon of salt
¼ teaspoon of freshly ground pepper

Cut the onions into rings and fry with the whole cloves of garlic in the butter until slightly browned. Add the washed organic nettles, the seasoning and water. Bring to the boil and simmer for five minutes.

Cream the soup in a liquidiser, bring to the boil and add more salt and pepper to taste.

To serve
Serve with a decent helping of whipped cream on top.

"In my native Sweden, nettles are dried over winter and crumbled into Rye bread. We have continued the practice of using nettles here in soup, which is a great favourite in the spring when the nettles are young."

Katherine Noren

dunworley cottage pork
in calvados marinade

"In Dunworley we 'grow' our own pigs and use the cutlets, etc. in the restaurant and other parts for salami and sausages."

SERVES 6

1 kg (2½ lb) pork chops, which provides approx. 6 average size chops

CALVADOS MARINADE
3 tablespoons of oil
1 tablespoon of fresh sage, chopped
salt and freshly ground pepper
¾ cup of calvados, or 1 bottle of cider mixed with 1¼ cup of brandy (to make about 1½ cups)
2 tablespoons of oil for frying

Marinade
First mix the marinade ingredients together, and pour over the pork chops.
Cover the pork chops and let them stand in a refrigerator overnight or for 2 nights if desired for extra flavour.

Frying
When the pork chops are ready, seal the juices in by frying in the oil over a high heat for 2 minutes. Then lower the heat and panfry for another 5 minutes. Serve immediately.

elderflower sorbet

Few seasons are more fleeting than that of Elderflower. They appear as suddenly as the first summer tourists and early May is not too soon to be ready for harvesting. Delay for too long and the best of the scent fades away, the blossoms begin to turn from cream to rust at the edges and it's "wait until next year".

SERVES 6

JUICE
60-80 elder flower heads
2 litres (3½ pints) boiling water
2 lemons
2 kg (4 lb) sugar
25 g (1 oz) citric acid

SORBET
2-3 egg whites

Sorbet
First you make the juice. Pick about 60-80 flower heads in blossom, best on a sunny day when the flowers are fully open. Put them in a large stainless steel bucket or similar vessel. Add the boiling water, zest from 2 lemons including the juice. Add the sugar and citric acid, stir, cover with muslin and leave for 3 days. Strain and the juice is ready. Mix with water for a refreshing summer drink or as a summer cocktail with champagne and strawberries.
Freeze about 300 ml (½ pint) of the juice. Do not freeze until solid. Meanwhile whisk 2-3 egg whites until firm and add to the semi-frozen juice without letting it defrost completely. Freeze again.

To serve
Once the mixture has refrozen serve in ice cold bowls.

mackerel with herbs and mushrooms

"The mackerel must be freshly caught and should be cooked as soon as possible. The good news is that any really fresh fish is good cooked this way. If you can get field mushrooms to go with them they will be superb. The green salad will need about three kinds of lettuce and other salad greens such as rocket, baby spinach leaves, cress, and a few fresh herbs. Access to a good garden is invaluable." Myrtle Allen

SERVES 4

4 very fresh mackerel, filleted
50 g (2 oz) of butter
seasoned flour

1 clove of garlic, crushed
225 g (8 oz) mushrooms, chopped
2 tablespoons of chopped fresh herbs
(thyme, parsley, chives, tarragon)
salt and freshly ground pepper

Dip the mackerel fillets in seasoned flour.
Heat the butter in a frying pan until foaming and fry the fillets until they are golden brown. Remove to a plate and keep warm.
Add the garlic, herbs and mushrooms to the pan and cook for a minute or two. Season to taste with salt and freshly ground pepper.

To serve
Divide the mackerel fillets between four warmed plates. Spoon the mushroom and herb mixture over the fillets and serve with fresh vegetables as available. Finely sliced runner beans and British Queen or Kerr's Pink potatoes would be seasonal and very good, and a good green salad.

GREEN SALAD
mixed salad leaves
1 teaspoon of a chopped
herb of your choice

Green salad
Wash the salad greens and tear into pieces that are not too small.
Sprinkle on a little herb of your choice.
For the dressing, beat the olive oil together with the salt, pepper and mustard and toss the greens in the dressing just before serving.

DRESSING
3 tablespoons of good olive oil or nut oil
a big pinch of salt
freshly ground pepper
¼ teaspoon of Dijon mustard

mackerel with herbs and mushrooms

Myrtle Allen opened her home, Ballymaloe House, as a restaurant in 1964 on
the Allen family farm. Under her inspired management, it became Ireland's foremost
country house hotel winning innumerable awards for its outstanding cuisine and
promotion of local Irish produce. Her influence on the development of cooking in
Cork has been enormous, including her aims of 'recapturing forgotten flavours and
preserving those that may soon die.' (Myrtle Allen from *The Ballymaloe Cookbook*)

tomato soup

SERVES 6

7 g (¼oz) of butter
50 g (2 oz) onion, finely chopped
900 g (2 lb) tomatoes
1 teaspoon of salt
1 teaspoon of sugar
a pinch of freshly ground
black pepper
500-600 ml (¾-1 pint) of fresh
chicken or vegetable stock

TO GARNISH
2-3 tablespoons of fresh cream
2 tablespoons of finely chopped
fresh basil or mint

The tomatoes you need must not just be ripe, but over-ripe and soft, and preferably not long life tomatoes. If you can peel them without scalding them first they will be perfect.

What is more, you should be able to buy them cheaply because tomorrow they will be no good! They should have a wonderful colour.

The onions must be freshly picked with the green stalk left on. Melt the butter in a heavy bottomed saucepan until it begins to foam.

Add the finely chopped onion, cover and sweat over a gentle heat until soft but not coloured.

Peel and halve the tomatoes and add them to the onion with a teaspoon each of salt and sugar, and a pinch of freshly ground black pepper.

Cover lightly and cook until the tomatoes are quite soft. When the tomatoes are cooked, either blend to a purée in a liquidiser or rub through a sieve.

Return to the saucepan and reheat adding the chicken or vegetable stock. Taste and adjust seasoning if necessary.

To serve
Pour the soup into warmed bowls or plates. Add a dash of cream to each bowl and scatter over some freshly chopped basil or mint. Serve piping hot.

crushed blueberries with cream

SERVES 4-5

500 g (1 lb) blueberries
350 g (12 oz) sugar

Preparation
Pound or mash together the ingredients until the fruit begins to break up.

Leave aside for a half an hour to allow the juice to run. They will keep in a fridge like this for a day or two.

To serve
Serve with cream or ice cream.

Myrtle Allen in the kitchen at Ballymaloe

roast chicken
with a courgette and herb stuffing

SERVES 4

I free range chicken

STUFFING
450 g (I lb) courgettes grated
60 g (2½ oz) unsalted butter
I medium onion peeled and
finely chopped
90 g (3 oz) cream cheese
60 g (2 oz) bread crumbs
25 g (I oz) parmesan
cheese freshly grated
I egg beaten
4 tablespoons of chopped fresh herbs
(tarragon, parsley and chervil)
sea salt and freshly ground black pepper

Preparation
To bone the chicken, place it upside down on the chopping board. With a sharp knife cut along the centre of the back bone and remove the carcass. Next, remove the thigh bones from the legs but leave drumsticks in place. (A friendly butcher might do this for you as it does require some skill.)

Stuffing
Top and tail the courgettes. Grate with the coarse side of a stainless steel grater. Salt them, let them stand for 20 minutes until the water oozes out, then squeeze or pat dry. Heat 13 g (½ oz) of the butter in a pan, add the finely chopped onion and sweat over a gentle heat until soft. Leave to cool.
Soften the remaining butter and blend with the cream cheese. Add half the breadcrumbs and work into the mixture.
Add the beaten egg, chopped herbs, onion and courgette and mix well.
Add the remaining breadcrumbs and the parmesan cheese. Season to taste with sea salt and freshly ground black pepper.

To cook the chicken
Preheat the oven to 200°C/400°F/gas mark 5.
Place the chicken, skin side up, flat on the roasting tin. Starting from the breast, use your fingers to loosen the skin away from the flesh. Gently push the stuffing through, first the legs and then the breast.
Tuck in the wings neatly. Season and sprinkle with olive oil.
Cook in the preheated oven for 40-50 minutes, basting frequently.

Note:
The herbs used above give a lovely summer flavour, but in winter you can use rosemary and thyme very successfully.

roast chicken with a courgette and herb stuffing

rich chocolate and nut cake

SERVES 8-10

175 g (6 oz) dark chocolate (must be
good quality, i.e. 55% cocoa solids)
175 g (6 oz) caster sugar
175 g (6 oz) unsalted butter
175 g (6 oz) ground hazelnuts
(which have been previously
roasted and skinned)
6 eggs (separated)

GLAZE
3 tablespoons of crab apple jelly
1 tablespoon of water

ICING
3 tablespoons crab apple jelly
100 g (3½ oz) dark chocolate
(broken into pieces)
100 g (3½ oz) cream

Preheat the oven to 180°C/350°F/gas mark 4.

Cake
Melt the chocolate and allow to cool.
Cream together 80 g (3 oz) of the sugar and butter. Mix
in the egg yolks and the cooled melted chocolate. Whisk
the egg whites into soft peaks and then whisk in the
remaining sugar.
Fold the nuts gently into the meringue. Then gently
combine the meringue with the chocolate mixture.
Turn into a 23 cm (9 in) spring-clip tin which has been
buttered.
Cook for approximately 40 minutes in the preheated
oven.
Allow to cool in the tin and then turn out onto a cooling
tray.

Glaze
Heat the crab apple jelly with 1 tablespoon of water and
brush over the cake.
Allow to cool.

Icing
Bring cream to the boil and whisk in the chocolate.
Allow to cool slightly. Then pour over top and sides of
the cake.

To serve
Decorate, if desired, with lemon balm leaves and whole
nuts.

This cake may be served as a dessert with a fruit
compote and vanilla ice cream or used as an afternoon
tea cake. It holds very well in a refrigerator for up to 4
days, and even improves with keeping.

The peaceful atmosphere of this North Cork 17th century house is further enhanced by a

fine reputation for hospitality and an excellent table d'hote. A walled kitchen garden

provides a range of the finest possible produce for the kitchen. Joe Bourke and his wife

Hazel are the second generation to oversee the restaurant since it first opened in 1965.

sautéed lambs' tongues
on a wholegrain mustard mash with tossed rocket leaves

SERVES 4

2 lambs' tongues
I small carrot, sliced
I small onion, peeled and chopped
½ a bay leaf
3 black peppercorns

WHOLEGRAIN MUSTARD MASH
2 floury potatoes
13 g (½oz) butter
I tablespoon of cream
I tablespoon of milk
I teaspoon of wholegrain mustard

SALAD
50 g (2 oz) rocket leaves
I tablespoon of French dressing

DRESSING
4 tablespoons of extra virgin olive oil
I tablespoon of non-scented oil
I tablespoon of white wine vinegar
a large pinch of salt
freshly ground pepper

COOKING THE TONGUE AND SAUCE
I tablespoon of olive oil
a knob of butter
the reserved tongue slices
salt and freshly ground pepper

200 ml (7 fluid oz) tongue stock
90 ml (3 fluid oz) fresh cream
I teaspoon of light soy sauce
salt and freshly ground pepper

Cooking the tongues
Wash the tongues thoroughly under cold running water. Put the vegetables in a large saucepan, sit the tongues on top and cover with cold water. Add the bay leaf and the peppercorns. Bring to the boil, lower the heat and simmer gently for 1 hour and 20 minutes.
Allow to cool, then lift out the tongues onto a chopping board lined with a tea towel and peel off the outer layer of skin, using a small paring knife. Slice thinly and remove to a plate.

Wholegrain mustard mash
Scrub the potatoes and cook them in boiling salted water in their jackets. When cooked, peel and mash. Add the butter, cream and milk and beat until light and fluffy. Stir in the wholegrain mustard and season to taste with salt and freshly ground pepper.

Salad
Wash and dry the rocket leaves. Put all the ingredients for the dressing into a small bowl and whisk well.

Cooking the tongue and sauce
Heat a heavy based frying pan until quite hot and add the butter and the oil. Put in the slices of lambs' tongues and toss for a few minutes until they are heated through, season with salt and freshly ground pepper and remove to a heated plate.

Remove the excess fat from the pan and pour in the tongue stock. Bring to the boil and reduce by two thirds. Add 1 teaspoon of light soy sauce and the cream and boil rapidly for a minute or two until it has reduced to a light coating consistency. Taste, and adjust seasoning if necessary.

To serve
Place a ring of wholegrain mustard mash in the centre of four warmed plates and arrange the slices of lambs tongues on top of the potato.
Toss the rocket leaves in 1 tablespoon of the French dressing and sit these on top of the tongue. Surround this centre piece with a few spoons of the sauce.

sautéed lambs' tongues on a wholegrain mustard mash with tossed rocket leaves

Prior to opening The Clean Slate Restaurant in Midleton in September 1997, chef Colm Falvey successfully ran the bistro style Earl of Orrery in Youghal. In his new minimalist designed restaurant he presents the same high standards. His Ballymaloe training is reflected in the use of fresh, seasonally available produce and in the contemporary twist with which he peppers French classic cooking.

monkfish panfried in garlic, chilli and fresh ginger
on a bed of blackened french beans

SERVES 4

4 x 175 g (6 oz) fillets of monkfish

450 g (1 lb) fine French beans
4 tablespoons of olive oil

salt and freshly ground pepper
175 g (6 oz) garlic butter
2 teaspoons of red chilli, finely diced
1 teaspoon of fresh ginger, finely grated
1 tablespoon of provençale tomato sauce
(see below)
1 tablespoon of fresh chives, finely chopped

TO GARNISH
deep fried straw potatoes
(1 potato peeled, cut into fine julienne
strips and deep fat fried)
4 sprigs of flat leaf parsley

PROVENÇALE TOMATO SAUCE
2 tablespoons extra virgin olive oil
1 medium onion, finely chopped
1 tin of Italian tomatoes, chopped
¼ teaspoon of sugar
1-2 cloves of garlic, peeled and crushed
1 tablespoon of chopped mixed fresh herbs
(basil, oregano, tarragon)
1 bay leaf
100 ml (3 fluid oz) dry white wine
salt and freshly ground pepper

Preparation
Cut the monkfish into circles approximately 1 cm
(¼ in) thick. Place on a plate and leave aside.

Blanch the beans by dropping them into a very large
pan of rapidly boiling salted water. Partially cook them,
drain and run cold water over them for 3-4 minutes.
Drain again and pat dry.

To cook
Heat a cast iron grill pan until it begins to smoke. Lay
the beans in a single layer in the pan, and drizzle with a
little olive oil. As they start to colour, turn them once by
rolling them over with a flat cooking utensil. Remove to
a plate and keep warm. Repeat the process until all the
beans are cooked.
Heat a heavy based frying pan until quite hot. Brush the
monkfish with the remaining olive oil and season with
salt and freshly ground black pepper.
Add the monkfish slices to the pan and sear for a few
seconds on each side until they are slightly brown. Turn
the heat to very low and add the garlic butter. Do not
allow it to burn.
Add the remaining ingredients, stir gently and cook for 2
minutes. Taste and adjust seasoning if necessary.

To serve
Have ready four warmed plates.
Lay the blackened beans in a criss-cross pattern around
the plates. Put the monkfish slices, stacked like a tower
in the centre and spoon the sauce over it. Top with
some deep fried straw potatoes and garnish with 4
sprigs of flat leaf parsley.

Provençale sauce
Heat the olive oil in a saucepan and sweat the onions
until they are tender but not browned. Stir in the
tomatoes, sugar, garlic, and herbs. Cover the pan and
cook slowly for 10 minutes. Remove the lid, add the
white wine and cook slowly for 30 minutes. Taste,
season with salt and freshly ground pepper, and pass
through a fine sieve. Reserve in a bowl and use as
needed.

dark chocolate marquise
wrapped in jacoude sponge with
roasted coconut and kirsch blackberries

JELLY
300 g (10 oz) blackberries
caster sugar to taste
4½ leaves of gelatine
1 measure of kirsch

JACOUDE SPONGE
3 egg whites
90 g (3 oz) sugar
3 egg yolks
40 g (1½ oz) flour
40 g (1½ oz) almonds
30 g (1 oz) melted butter - unsalted

CHOCOLATE MARQUISE
200 g (7 oz) dark chocolate
(55% cocoa solids)
75 g (3 oz) honey
1 tablespoon diluted coffee
400 ml (13 fluid oz)
semi whipped cream
70 g (2½ oz) unsalted butter
3 egg yolks

SERVING DECORATION
sugar syrup - equal quantities of
sugar and water boiled for a couple
of minutes and then allowed to
cool (can be stored)
1 packet of desiccated coconut,
toasted under a hot grill

Preheat the oven to 180°C/350°F/gas mark 4.

Preparation
Grease a flat baking tray with butter and then line with a sheet of baking parchment.

Jelly
Bring the blackberries and kirsch slowly to the boil. Add sugar to taste, liquidise and then pass through a fine sieve. Soak the gelatine in cold water until soft and add to the blackberries. Place in the refrigerator until cool.

Jacoude sponge
Cream half the sugar with the 3 egg yolks, then add the melted butter. Mix the flour and almonds and add to eggs and sugar. Whisk the egg whites with remaining sugar and fold into the sponge mixture. Spread the mixture as thinly as possible on the prepared tray. Cook for 4-6 minutes in the preheated oven. Once cooked turn onto a cooling rack and cover with a damp cloth.

Chocolate marquise
Combine chocolate, honey, diluted coffee and butter in a bowl over a pot of simmering water. When mixture has melted together, place bowl over a pot of iced water and stir. When cool, whisk in the egg yolks. Then fold in the semi-whipped cream.

To assemble
Place a sheet of grease-proof paper on a flat surface and dust with icing sugar. Lay the Jacoude sponge on this. Spread the marquise mixture lightly over the sponge. Cut the blackberry jelly into stripes and place a line of jelly down the middle of the marquise. Then carefully roll them into a roulade and place in the refrigerator.

To serve
When set, roll the outside of the sponge in a light film of sugar syrup and then into the toasted coconut.

"First-time customers sometimes look at me with shock when I ask - Would you like to take the menu to Levis's pub across the road, and I'll come and get your order there?"

pan fried monkfish with a tangy lemon sauce

SERVES 4

THE FISH
1 kg (2½ lb) monkfish,
skinned, centre bone removed
and cut into large bite sized chunks
white flour seasoned
with salt and freshly
ground black pepper

LEMON SAUCE
make ahead of time if you wish as
the fish only takes a few minutes
25 g (1 oz) butter
1 small onion peeled and
finely chopped
zest and juice of 2 lemons
250 ml (8 fluid oz) white wine
125 ml (4 fluid oz) fish stock
125 ml (4 fluid oz) fresh cream
salt and freshly
ground black pepper

Toss the chunks of monkfish in the seasoned flour until well coated. Shake off the excess and reserve. Use 1 part olive oil and 1 part vegetable oil to coat the base of a large frying pan.

Lemon sauce
Melt the butter in a wide based saucepan, add the onions and sweat over a gentle heat until they are soft.
Add the zest and juice of the lemons, the white wine and the fish stock.
Bring to the boil and boil rapidly to reduce the liquid by two thirds.
Pour in the cream, bring to the boil again and reduce to a consistency thick enough to coat the back of a spoon.
Taste, and season with salt and freshly ground black pepper.

To cook the fish
Heat the prepared frying pan over a moderately high heat. Cook the monkfish pieces quickly turning each piece as it becomes crisp and golden.

To serve
Drain the fish on kitchen paper and serve immediately on warmed plates with a small bowl of the tangy lemon sauce.
Garnish each plate with a segment of lemon and a sprig of parsley.

Delicious with creamy mashed potatoes!

pan fried monkfish with a tangy lemon sauce

baked avocado with crab meat

SERVES 4

I avocado peeled and chopped
225 g (8 oz) white crab meat
8 crab toes cooked (if available)
150 ml (¼ pint)
seasoned béchamel sauce (recipe below)
50 g (2 oz) cheddar cheese, grated

BÉCHAMEL SAUCE
300 ml (½ pint) milk
a few slices of carrot
a few slices of onion
3 peppercorns
small sprig of thyme
small sprig of parsley
40 g (½ oz) roux
(equal quantities of butter and flour
cooked together for 2 minutes
over a gentle heat)
salt and freshly ground
black pepper

TO GARNISH
4 parsley sprigs
4 wedges of lemon

Grease 4 ovenproof ramekin dishes.
Preheat the oven to 200°C/400°F/gas mark 6.

Divide the crab meat between the 4 ramekin dishes. In each dish place 2 crab toes, with points facing upwards (one at each side).
Divide the chopped avocado and pile on top of the crab meat.
Pour over enough béchamel sauce to generously coat the mixture.
Top with the grated cheese.
Bake in the preheated oven for 15 minutes or until a golden crust forms on top.

Béchamel sauce
Put the cold milk into a saucepan with the carrot, onion, thyme, peppercorns and parsley.
Bring to the boil, lower the heat and simmer for 4-5 minutes.
Remove from the heat and leave to infuse for 10 minutes.
Strain out the vegetables. Bring the milk back to the boil and thicken to a light coating consistency by whisking in the roux.
Season to taste with salt and freshly ground black pepper.

To serve
Garnish each dish with a lemon wedge and a sprig of parsley and serve immediately.

fresh orange soufflé

SERVES 4-6

Preheat the oven to 220°C/425°F/gas mark 7.

PASTRY CREAM
250 ml (8 fluid oz) milk
3 egg yolks
100 g (3½ oz) sugar
30 g (1 oz) flour

Pastry Cream
Heat the milk in a saucepan. Combine the egg yolks,
sugar and flour in a separate saucepan.
Pour hot milk onto the egg mixture, slowly at first,
whisking all the time.
Stir over a low heat until the pastry cream is thick and
cooked.
Keep until needed.

FRESH ORANGE SOUFFLÉ
2 oranges
75 ml (2½ fluid oz) Grand Marnier
5 egg whites
30 g (1 oz) caster sugar
icing sugar for sieving

Soufflé
Grate the rind of 1 orange and stir into the pastry cream
with 3 tablespoons of Grand Marnier.
Peel and section 2 oranges and sprinkle with remaining
Grand Marnier.
Prepare a soufflé dish by rubbing the inside lightly with
butter. Wrap a band of doubled grease proof paper
around the dish to stand 5-7 cm (2-3 in) above the rim.
This will give the soufflé extra height to rise.
Heat pastry cream until hot to touch.
Beat egg whites, add caster sugar and mix to a light
meringue. Fold this mix into pastry cream.
Turn half into prepared dish, set orange segments on
top and add remaining mix.

Tip:
When you fill the soufflé dish, run your thumb around
the edge of the dish so that the soufflé will rise in a hat
shape.

Bake in the preheated oven until well risen or puffed
and brown (12-15 minutes). Then draw out oven shelf
with soufflé on it, dust top quickly with icing sugar, and
return to the oven.
Cook for a further 4-5 minutes to caramelise the top.

To serve
Once you remove this dessert from the oven, serve at
once.

angel hair pasta with artichokes, sun-dried tomatoes and chilli

SERVES 2

225 g (8 oz) angel hair pasta
(egg vermicelli)
1 teaspoon of salt

2 dessertspoons of
extra virgin olive oil
6 artichoke hearts, drained and cut in half
(good quality canned or fresh)
2 garlic cloves, peeled and crushed
3 anchovy fillets, finely chopped
3 teaspoons of chilli oil (or to taste)
6 pieces of sundried tomato,
cut in strips
squeeze of lemon juice to taste
2 dessertspoons of mixed fresh herbs,
roughly chopped (rosemary or sage
mixed with flat leaf parsley)
freshly grated parmesan

GARNISH
13 g (½ oz) freshly grated parmesan
2 sprigs of whichever
herb used in the dish

Cook the pasta in plenty of boiling salted water until al dente.

Meanwhile, heat the olive oil in a stainless steel low sided pan and sauté the artichokes hearts with the garlic and anchovies for a few minutes.
Add the chilli oil, the sundried tomatoes and the lemon juice, and cook for another minute or two, stirring continuously. Take off the heat while you drain the pasta.

Add the steaming hot pasta to the artichoke mixture, sprinkle on the 25 g (1 oz) of freshly grated parmesan and the freshly chopped herbs and toss well. Taste and adjust seasoning with salt and freshly ground pepper if necessary.
(Remember the anchovies will add quite a bit of salt to the dish so you may not need to add any at this stage.)

To serve
Divide between two warm plates, scatter the remaining parmesan over the pasta and garnish with a sprig of herb.

angel hair pasta with artichokes, sun-dried tomatoes and chilli

Adele's, at the top of the main street in Schull, is a bakery and café, run by Adele O'Connor. She is famed far and wide for the wonderful breads, cakes and scones which are baked using her own recipes. Adele's son, Simon O'Connor is also working there and a full dinner menu is now available in the evenings.

salmon with black peppercorn vinaigrette

SERVES 4-6

MARINADE
I teaspoon of black peppercorns
75 ml (2½ fluid oz) good quality white
wine vinegar

SALMON
900 g (2 lb) fresh salmon fillets, skinned
coarse sea salt to taste

POACHING LIQUID
75 ml (2½ fluid oz) dry white wine

VINAIGRETTE
120 ml (4 fluid oz) extra virgin olive oil
marinade mixture from above
sea salt to taste

GARNISH
12 chive flowers

Crush the peppercorns coarsely with a mortar and pestle and put them along with the wine vinegar into a small earthenware bowl. Cover with cling film and allow to marinate for 2 hours or more.

Salmon
Preheat the oven to 230°C/450°F/gas mark 7.
Place the salmon fillets on a tray and remove any bones with pliers or pinchers. Cut diagonally into strips 2.5 cm (1 in) wide.
Lightly oil a shallow roasting tin (non-reactive) and cut a piece of oiled grease proof paper to fit snugly inside it. Season the salmon strips with the salt and place them in the roasting tin. Pour over the white wine and cover with the grease-proof paper. Poach in the preheated oven for 7-10 minutes.
Remove from the oven and allow to cool in the roasting tin.

Vinaigrette
Combine the olive oil with the vinegar and crushed peppercorn marinade in a bowl and mix well. Season to taste with sea salt.

To serve
Place 1-2 pieces of salmon on each plate and spoon over a little of the vinaigrette with some of the black peppercorns.
Garnish with the chive flowers.

lemon cake

SERVES 8

CAKE MIXTURE
125 g (4 oz) margarine
3 eggs
125 g (4 oz) caster sugar
125 g (4 oz) plain white flour
I level teaspoon baking powder
grated rind of ½ lemon

SYRUP
125 g (4 oz) caster sugar
150 ml (¼ pint) water
juice of I lemon
grated rind of ½ lemon

GLACÉ ICING
250 g (8 oz) icing sugar sieved
2-3 tablespoons lemon juice
grated rind of ½ lemon

Preheat the oven to 175°C/350°F/gas mark 4.

Cream the margarine and sugar
Add eggs, one at a time, beating after each one.
Add a little flour with the last egg, to prevent
curdling.
Fold in the flour which has been sieved with the
baking powder.
Put into a greased and lined 20 cm (8 in) round tin
and bake.
When the cake is cooked, leave to cool for 10
minutes, then remove carefully and place on a
large plate.

Syrup
Put all the ingredients into a saucepan and stir
over a low heat until the sugar has dissolved.

Icing
Place the sieved icing sugar and lemon rind in a
bowl. Stir in enough lemon juice to make a very
stiff icing.
Spread the icing carefully over the top. The icing
will even out by itself.
Tip: Don't be tempted to spread it too much as the
surface of the cake may lift off.

irish rock oysters with angel hair pasta
and a chilli, garlic and oyster sauce

SERVES 4

12 large rock oysters (Pacific)

375 g (13 oz) angel hair pasta
(egg vermicelli)

SAUCE
20 ml (½ fluid oz) peanut oil
2 shallots finely chopped
20 g (¾ oz) root ginger
peeled and grated
2 cloves of garlic peeled
and finely chopped
100 ml (3 fluid oz)
real oyster sauce
60 ml (2 fluid oz) chilli sauce
150 ml (5 fluid oz) double cream
salt and freshly ground pepper

Native Irish Oysters are best when there is an 'r' in the month. Imported Pacific oysters are available all year round.

Preparing the oysters
Open the oysters and detach completely from their shells. Using a plastic sieve strain the shuked oysters (oysters taken out of their shells) into a non-metallic bowl or basin, and reserve the oyster juice.
Wash and scrub the shells well and leave aside.

Pasta
Bring a large pot of salted water to the boil and cook the pasta as directed on the packet. Drain in a colander and reserve.

Sauce
Heat a medium sized sauté or frying pan over a moderate heat, pour in the peanut oil, add the ginger and shallots and cook gently for 2 minutes.
Add the garlic and cook for a further 1-2 minutes.
When the shallot mixture is cooked, add the oyster and chilli sauces and the double cream, and stir well, but do not boil.
Taste and adjust seasoning with salt and freshly ground pepper. Reserve and keep warm.

To finish
Pour the oyster juice into the same pan that the pasta was cooked in. Season with freshly ground black pepper and bring to the boil. Add the reserved pasta to this and heat through.

Add the oysters to the reserved sauce and heat gently until they stiffen. Be extremely careful not to overcook them

To serve
Warm 4 large plates and 12 oyster shells.
Arrange 3 warmed oyster shells on each plate. Divide the pasta between the shells and top with the oyster sauce. Serve immediately.

The Oysterhaven is a cottage restaurant at the crossroads between
Oysterhaven, Kinsale and Cork. In the last ten years Chef/Proprietor
Bill Patterson and his wife Sylvia built up a loyal following who
relished the creative flair Bill brought to French classic cuisine.

medallion of beef
with cashel blue cheese and port wine sauce

"This is a dish which can be prepared easily at home as no stock making is required. For this recipe I use Cashel Blue, a creamy blue cheese from Cashel, County Tipperary, but you may substitute this with any good blue cheese, for example, Stilton. I also like to use large plump golden sultanas soaked overnight in port."

SERVES 4

Steaks

4 trimmed fillet steaks each weighing approx. 175 g (6 oz)

2 tablespoons of olive oil

2 shallots finely chopped

salt and freshly ground pepper

200 g (7 oz) Cashel Blue cheese

SAUCE

3 tablespoons of water

80 g (3 oz) golden sultanas soaked overnight in 200 ml (7 fluid oz) port

100 g (3½ oz) roasted pine nuts

100 g (3½ oz) chilled unsalted butter, cut into cubes

1 dessertspoon Dijon mustard

sea salt and freshly ground black pepper

½ a lemon

GARNISH

1 bunch of fresh dill finely chopped

To cook the steaks
Brush the steaks with the olive oil and leave aside. Heat a heavy based frying pan over a medium high heat until it begins to smoke. Add the steaks and cook for approximately 5-8 minutes according to your liking. Remove to a warmed plate, sprinkle with the shallots and season with salt and freshly ground pepper. Cover and keep warm.
Leave to rest for at least 5 minutes before serving.

The sauce
Using the same pan, de-glaze with the water, and boil rapidly until the liquid is reduced by two thirds.
Add the sultanas and port, stir to dissolve the caramelised meat juices, then add the pine nuts.
Lower the heat and whisking gently, add the butter cubes, a few at a time, until the sauce thickens to a syrupy consistency.
Add the Dijon mustard and any juices which have collected from the steaks.
Taste and adjust seasoning if necessary. Complete the sauce with a squeeze of lemon juice.

To serve
Preheat the grill to high. Top the steaks with a slice of Cashel Blue cheese and place under the grill to brown. Put a steak in the centre of each of the warmed plates, and spoon the port wine sauce around the steaks. Serve immediately with a crisp green salad and a few potatoes tossed in good olive oil and some freshly chopped dill.

medallion of beef
with cashel blue cheese
and port wine sauce

fresh crab cakes

SERVES 4

1 large free range egg
1½ tablespoons of cream
1½ teaspoons Dijon mustard
1 teaspoon Worcestershire sauce
a pinch of cayenne pepper
salt and freshly ground white pepper

1½ tablespoons of parsley
or dill finely chopped
1½ tablespoons of spring
onion finely chopped
4 tablespoons of home-made mayonnaise

450 g (1 lb) white crab meat
1½ tablespoons ground almonds

COATING
seasoned flour
1 free range egg white, beaten
50 g (2 oz) fresh white breadcrumbs

125 g (4 oz) clarified butter or
sunflower oil to fry the crab cakes

Preparation
Break the egg into a large bowl and whisk lightly with a fork. Add the cream, mustard, Worcestershire sauce, cayenne pepper, salt and freshly ground pepper and mix well.
Stir in the chopped parsley, spring onions and mayonnaise.
Gently fold in the crab meat and ground almonds. When well incorporated, wet your hands and form the mixture into four equal-sized cakes.

Coat each cake, first with seasoned flour, then egg and finally breadcrumbs. Place on a baking tray lined with silicone paper, cover with cling film and chill in the refrigerator for approximately 1 hour.

To cook the crab cakes
Heat the clarified butter or oil in a non-stick frying pan. (Note: to clarify butter refer to method in Medallions of Venison recipe.)
Cook the crab cakes over a moderate heat until crisp and golden (approximately 3-4 minutes each side).
Drain on kitchen paper.

Serving suggestion
Serve garnished with a tossed green salad and some home-made tartare sauce, or a nice salsa.

breast of chicken
marinated in lemon, garlic and chilli
with white wine and basil sauce

SERVES 4

4 chicken breasts, preferably
free range, flattened out slightly

MARINADE

zest and juice of 2 lemons
4 teaspoons of chilli oil or
1 small red chilli finely chopped
2 tablespoons of olive oil
salt and freshly ground black pepper

SAUCE

25 g (1 oz) butter
4 shallots peeled and
finely chopped
8 button mushrooms washed
and finely chopped
1 clove of garlic crushed
1 sprig of thyme
170 ml (6 fluid oz) dry white wine
475 ml (14 fluid oz) chicken stock
170 ml (6 fluid oz) fresh cream
salt and freshly ground black pepper
1 bunch of fresh basil, chopped

GARNISH

basil oil
fresh basil leaves

Marinade
Put all the ingredients for the marinade into a bowl and
mix well.
Toss the chicken breasts in this mixture, cover with cling
film and leave to marinate in the refrigerator for up to 1
hour.

Sauce
Melt the butter in a saucepan until it begins to foam. Add
the shallots, mushrooms, garlic and thyme and sauté gently
until they turn golden brown.
Pour in the white wine, bring to the boil and reduce until it
has almost evaporated.
Add the chicken stock, bring to the boil again, and reduce
by half.
Finally, add the cream, and boil rapidly until the sauce
reaches a light coating consistency.
Taste and adjust seasoning. Pour through a fine sieve into
a clean saucepan and reserve.

To cook the chicken
Heat a cast iron grill pan until quite hot and brush with a
little olive oil. Cook the chicken breasts until just cooked
through, golden, and well marked on both sides
(approximately 8-10 minutes).

To serve
Reheat the sauce and stir in the freshly chopped basil.
Spoon a little sauce into the centre of four warmed plates
and arrange a chicken breast on top of the sauce. Drizzle
over a little basil oil if you have it and garnish with some
fresh basil leaves.
Serve with a good tossed salad and some rustic potatoes.

iced coffee and praline parfait with an Irish coffee sauce

iced coffee and praline parfait
with an irish coffee sauce

SERVES 8-10

PARFAIT
2 egg whites
175 g (6 oz) caster sugar
6 tablespoons water
3 tablespoons strong black coffee
1 tablespoon Grand Marnier
350 g (12 oz) lightly whipped cream

PRALINE FILLING
50 g (2 oz) unblanched almonds
50 g (2 oz) caster sugar

IRISH COFFEE SAUCE
250 g (8 oz) caster sugar
70 ml (3 fluid oz) water
250 ml (8 fluid oz) strong coffee
1 tablespoon Irish whiskey

Dissolve the sugar in the water over a gentle heat. Bring to the boil for 3 minutes.

Whisk the egg whites until stiff, then pour sugar mixture on to the egg whites slowly, whisking constantly at high speed. Continue whisking until cool.

Add in the coffee and Grand Marnier and finally fold in the whipped cream.

Praline filling
Heat almonds and sugar gently in a small heavy pan. When sugar is a liquid caramel, stir carefully with a metal spoon to toast nuts on all sides. Turn on to an oiled tin and leave to set.

When cold, crush the praline with a rolling pin.

Line a 1 kg (2 lb) loaf tin with cling film. Spoon half the parfait mixture into the lined loaf tin, cover with a layer of crushed praline and finally the remaining mixture, finishing with a covering of praline on top. Freeze for 4 — 6 hours or overnight.

Sauce
Dissolve the sugar in the water. Bring to the boil and boil until the syrup resembles chestnut coloured caramel. Add the coffee and allow to cool. Finally, add the Irish whiskey and serve with the parfait.

Since 1994 Gregory's has been a welcome addition to the culinary life of Carrigaline, a growing suburb of Cork city. The menus feature fresh local produce and are changed regularly to reflect produce which is in season.

vegetable ragout

SERVES 4

40 ml (1½ fluid oz) of vegetable
or olive oil
400 g (14 oz) mushrooms
400 g (14 oz) carrots
400 g (14 oz) courgettes
2 litres of water
1 teaspoon of salt
200 ml (7 fluid oz) fresh cream
salt and freshly ground pepper

Preparation
Wash the mushrooms and pat dry with kitchen paper.
Chop them finely and leave aside.
Peel and cut the carrots into thumb sized pieces and
then into julienne strips.
Cut the courgettes in the same way and place each of
the vegetables on separate plates.

Cooking the vegetables
Heat the vegetable oil in a heavy frying pan over a
medium heat.
Add the finely chopped mushrooms and cook until they
are reduced to almost nothing - this is achieved by
allowing the mushrooms to release their liquid and
evaporate fully. The mushrooms become crisp and
brown retaining an enhanced mushroom flavour.
Remove to a plate.

Put the 2 litres of water into a large saucepan with the
salt and bring to the boil.
Add the carrots and cook until tender but still firm.
Remove from the boiling water with a slotted spoon and
plunge into cold water until completely cold.
Drain and refrigerate until needed.
Bring the water to the boil again, add the courgettes,
bring back to the boil and remove immediately.
Plunge into cold water and drain as before.

To serve
Heat the mushrooms in a saucepan, pour in the cream
and bring to the boil. Add the drained carrots and
courgettes and heat everything through.
Season to taste with salt and freshly ground pepper.
Divide the mixture between four warmed plates, piling
the vegetables in the centre, and allowing the juices to
spread around the vegetables.
Serve immediately.

The enjoyable experience offered by this restaurant on Heir Island in Roaring Water Bay, begins as soon as you step from the slipway into the ferry boat at Cunnamore Pier. Here, you encounter some of your fellow diners who will also partake of a menu featuring the freshest local organic and wild island ingredients of that day in a very unique and beautiful setting. Guests will be pleased to note the ferryboat is larger than John Desmond's fishing boat, shown here.

117

duck breasts with a lemon sauce,
lemon confit, roast potatoes, carrot and orange purée

SERVES 4

4 duck breasts
each weighing approximately 350 g (12 oz)

ROAST POTATOES
900 g (2 lb) medium potatoes
duck fat or olive oil

CARROT AND ORANGE PURÉE
450 g (1 lb) carrots
2 strips of orange zest
2 tablespoons of double cream

LEMON CONFIT
zest of 1 lemon
50 g (2 oz) sugar

LEMON SAUCE
50 g (2 oz) sugar
50 ml (2 fluid oz) cold water
juice of 1 lemon
200 ml (7 fluid oz) reduced
duck or chicken stock
50 g (2 oz) butter, cold and diced
salt and freshly ground pepper

Preheat the oven to 230°C/450°F/gas mark 8.

Roast potatoes
Wash and peel the potatoes, put into a steamer and cook
until tender. Remove and allow to cool.
Heat the duck fat or olive oil in a fireproof roasting dish,
add the potatoes, some salt and freshly ground pepper
and toss in the fat.
Roast in the preheated oven for 20 minutes.

Carrot and orange purée
Top and tail and scrape or thinly peel the carrots, then
slice into thick rounds.
Put into a saucepan with the strips of orange zest and a
pinch of salt, and barely cover with cold water.
Bring to the boil, and cook until tender and the water
has evaporated. Remove the orange zest, add the cream
and heat through.
Purée in either a food processor or a blender.
Return to the saucepan, taste, season, then re-heat
stirring.
Keep warm.

Lemon confit
Cut the zest of 1 lemon into julienne strips and put it
into a small stainless steel saucepan.
Cover with cold water and bring to the boil, strain, and
return the zest to the saucepan.
Again, cover with cold water, add the sugar, bring to the
boil and simmer, uncovered, until the liquid is reduced.
Reserve.

Lemon sauce
Put the sugar and cold water in a heavy based saucepan.
Heat gently until the sugar has dissolved. Raise the heat
high and cook until golden caramel. Brush down the
sides of the pan with a pastry brush dipped in cold
water a few times as it is boiling. This prevents the
caramel from crystallizing.
Add the juice of 1 lemon and the reduced duck stock.
Bring to the boil and at the last minute whisk in the cold
diced butter.
Taste and adjust seasoning.

Duck
Place the duck breasts, skin side down in a large heated
frying pan.
Cook gently for approximately 10 minutes, discard the
surplus fat during cooking. Increase the heat and cook
the other side for approximately 5 minutes.
Remove, and keep warm.
They should be left to rest for about 15 minutes. Pour
any cooking juices into the lemon sauce.

To serve
Put a portion of carrot purée in the centre of four
warmed plates. Slice the duck breasts thinly and fan the
slices on top of the carrot. Spoon the sauce over the
duck and garnish with the lemon confit.
Surround with the roast potatoes, and serve.

timbale of gravlax salmon and beansprout
coated with an anise cream and lemon vinaigrette

SERVES 6

450 g (1 lb) wild salmon fillet
125 g (4 oz) coarse sea salt

MARINADE
zest of 1 lemon
zest of ½ lime
zest of ½ orange
13 g (½ oz) of chopped fresh dill
5 coriander seeds, crushed
¼ teaspoon of crushed
Chinese red pepper
1 tablespoon of olive oil

ANISE CREAM
100 ml (3½ fluid oz) fresh cream
1 dessertspoon of
Ricard vermouth, or Pernod
salt and freshly ground pepper

VINAIGRETTE
150 ml (¼ pint) olive oil
juices of the lemon,
½ lime and ½ orange
½ teaspoon of sugar
½ teaspoon of salt

TO ASSEMBLE
50 g (2 oz) bean sprouts
¼ cucumber, thinly sliced
a pinch of salt

GARNISH
a few cubes of salmon
reserved from above
6 sprigs of fresh dill

Place the prepared salmon on a tray and remove any bones with pliers or pinchers. Cover the flesh side with the coarse salt and leave to marinate for 6 hours. Wash off the salt for 1 hour in cold running water and leave to dry on a towel overnight.

Marinade
Grate the zest of the lemon, orange and the lime into a bowl. Add the chopped dill, the crushed coriander, the crushed Chinese red pepper and the olive oil and mix well. Rub this paste into the flesh side of the salmon and leave it to rest for several hours.

Anise cream
Pour the cream into a bowl and whip until it forms soft peaks. Season with salt and freshly ground pepper and stir in the Pernod.

Vinaigrette
Whisk the oil and juices together in a bowl to emulsify. Add the sugar, the salt and freshly ground pepper and mix well.

The cucumber
Slice the cucumber thinly, place in a colander, sprinkle with salt and leave for 30 minutes to remove the indigestible acids. Before use, rinse under cold running water, pat dry and leave aside on a plate.

To assemble
Cut the salmon into 3 mm (½ in) square cubes, put it into a bowl and season with freshly ground black pepper. (In a separate bowl reserve a few cubes of salmon for the garnish and leave aside.) Add the bean sprouts and mix well. Have ready 6 small white plates and a ring mould 5 x 3.5 cm (2 x 1½   in). Place the ring in the centre of a plate and fill it nine-tenths full with the salmon. Press down gently with the back of a teaspoon.
Spoon the cream into the top of the mould and smooth over with a spatula. Carefully lift off the ring mould. Repeat the process for the remaining five timbales.

To serve
Surround the base of the salmon timbales with overlapping slices of cucumber. Season the cucumber with a little salt and spoon some vinaigrette over and around the slices. Garnish each one with a few cubes of the reserved salmon and a sprig of dill. Serve immediately.

In 1967 the O'Callaghan family opened their listed Georgian House overlooking the famous Blackwater River as a country house hotel. Since then the river has been a source of superb fish dishes, as well as peace and inspiration for both guests and chef William O'Callaghan. Self-sufficiency is a hallmark of Longueville, achieved through their farm and garden's supply of lamb, fruit and vegetables and complemented by white wines from their own vineyard - when Irish growing conditions allow.

The conservatory at Longueville House.

mussels gratinated with herb breadcrumbs
and served with a vierge sauce

SERVES 8

MUSSELS
3 kg (½ stone) mussels
a knob of butter
½ medium onion,
peeled and finely chopped
1 carrot, sliced
1 sprig of parsley
1 sprig of thyme
1 glass of wine

VIERGE SAUCE
100 ml (3½ fluid oz) olive oil
1 teaspoon of lemon juice
1 teaspoon of lemon zest
salt and freshly ground pepper
2 tomatoes, skinned and de-seeded
1 teaspoon of freshly chopped basil

TOMATO SAUCE
(alternative option)
6 tomatoes
1 dessertspoon of olive oil
½ a fennel bulb, finely chopped
1 medium onion,
peeled and finely chopped
1 sprig of thyme
1 star of anise
reserved mussel juice
salt and freshly ground pepper
pinch of sugar

BREADCRUMBS
4 slices of stale bread
1 sprig of thyme
2 tablespoons of chopped parsley
1 sprig of rosemary
1 sprig of fennel
1½ tablespoons of olive oil

These mussels can be served with a variety of sauces. Included here is an option for a hot tomato sauce which is interchangeable with the above.

To cook the mussels
Melt the butter in a heavy-based saucepan and sweat the vegetables and herbs over a gentle heat until soft but not coloured.
Meanwhile, check that all the mussels are tightly closed, wash them and remove the beards.
When the vegetables are cooked, add the mussels and the white wine, cover with a lid and cook over a medium heat, shaking the pan occasionally. As soon as the shells open, remove from the heat and discard any that remain closed. Strain the juices from the mussels into a small bowl through a fine sieve or cloth and reserve.
Remove the mussels from their shells, put them into a separate bowl and keep warm.

Vierge sauce
Slice the lemon zest into fine julienne strips and blanch in boiling water for about 5 minutes. Drain and refresh under cold running water.
Leave to drain on kitchen paper.
Combine the olive oil, lemon juice and zest, salt and freshly ground pepper in a bowl and whisk well. Stir in the diced tomatoes and the basil.

Tomato sauce (an alternative option)
Remove the hard core from the tomatoes, put them into a deep bowl and cover with boiling water. Count to 10 and pour off the water immediately. Peel off the skins starting from the stem hole and cut them in half crosswise, not through the stem. Squeeze each half gently to extract the seeds and juices and chop roughly.

Heat the olive oil in a saucepan, add the chopped vegetables and sweat over a gentle heat until soft. Add the chopped tomatoes, thyme, star of anise and mussel juice. Bring to the boil, reduce the heat and simmer gently for 15 minutes. Season to

mussels gratinated with herb breadcrumbs and served with a vierge sauce

taste with salt, freshly ground black pepper and a pinch of sugar if necessary.
Empty the contents of the saucepan into a liquidiser and blend until smooth. Return to
the saucepan and reserve.

Breadcrumbs
Cut the crusts off the stale white bread and whizz the soft part of the bread in the
liquidiser or food processor for a few seconds. Remove to a bowl and add the chopped
herbs and olive oil. Mix well.

To assemble
Place 8 greased stainless steel ring moulds 5 x 7.5 cm (2 x 3 in) on a baking tray.
Season the warm mussels and press them into the moulds with the back of a teaspoon,
leaving enough space for the breadcrumbs at the top.
Evenly distribute the breadcrumbs over the top of the mussels and place them under a
hot grill until they turn a light golden brown.

To serve
Have ready 8 warmed plates.
Place a mould in the centre of each plate and carefully lift off the rings. Spoon
some of the vierge sauce around the mussels, or alternatively, reheat the tomato sauce
and replace the vierge with this. Serve immediately.

escalope of roasted sea fresh cod

with a sundried tomato tapenade crust on a bed of orange and caper ratatouille with roasted yellow pepper coulis

SERVES 4

TAPENADE CRUST

1 bunch of fresh basil - chopped
50 g (2 oz) stoned black olives
25 g (1 oz) anchovies
1 teaspoon of capers, washed
1 teaspoon of coarse grain mustard
1 teaspoon of freshly ground black pepper
50 g (2 oz) semi sun-dried tomatoes
1 teaspoon of crushed garlic

25 ml (1 fluid oz) olive oil
50 g (2 oz) fresh white breadcrumbs

ORANGE AND CAPER RATATOUILLE

1 small tin plum tomatoes 250 g (9 oz)
25 ml (1 fluid oz) of best quality olive oil
4 shallots peeled and finely chopped
2 red peppers, skinned and diced (5 mm)
2 yellow peppers, skinned and diced (5 mm)
1 small aubergine diced (5 mm)
200 g (7 oz) courgettes diced (5 mm)
1 ripe plum tomato, skinned, seeded and diced (5 mm)
25 g (1 oz) small capers, washed
zest and juice of 1 orange
salt and freshly ground black pepper

ROASTED YELLOW PEPPER COULIS

4 ripe yellow peppers
olive oil for drizzling over the peppers
1 tablespoon of olive oil
2 shallots peeled and finely chopped
120 ml (4 fluid oz) fresh vegetable stock
40 ml (1½ fluid oz) olive oil
1 teaspoon truffle oil (optional)
freshly ground sea salt
freshly ground black pepper

Tapenade crust
Put all the ingredients except the olive oil and breadcrumbs into a food processor and purée for two minutes until it forms a thick paste.
Adjust the speed setting to slow and add the olive oil and breadcrumbs. This will give you a rough paste.

Orange and caper ratatouille
Empty the can of tomatoes into a liquidiser and purée until smooth. Using a wooden spoon, force the tomato pulp through a fine sieve into a bowl and reserve.
Heat the olive oil in a large pan over a moderate heat. Put in the shallots and sweat for two minutes. Add the peppers, aubergine and courgettes and cook over a gentle heat for a further five minutes.
Add the sieved tomato, the diced plum tomato, the orange juice and zest, and finally, the capers. Allow this mixture to simmer for a further 8-10 minutes until the liquids have reduced by half.
Taste and adjust the seasoning with salt and freshly ground black pepper. Keep warm.

Yellow pepper coulis
Preheat the oven to 230°C/450°F/gas mark 8.
Drizzle a little olive oil over the peppers and bake in the preheated oven for 8-10 minutes until the skin darkens and begins to blister. Remove from the oven and place in a bowl. Cover with cling film and leave for 10-15 minutes. This will make them much easier to peel. Remove the skin, seeds and stalks from the peppers and roughly chop the flesh. Reserve.
Heat 1 tablespoon of olive oil in a large pan over a moderate heat. Add the shallots and sweat gently until they are soft. Add the chopped yellow pepper and cook for a further two minutes. Add the vegetable stock, bring to the boil, reduce the heat and simmer for 15 minutes. When cooked pour the contents of the saucepan into a liquidiser and blitz for 1 minute to give a sauce consistency. Push the mixture through a fine sieve into a clean bowl.
Rinse the liquidiser goblet and return the contents of the bowl to it. With the motor running slowly this time, liquidise the mixture again adding the olive oil and truffle

escalope of roasted sea fresh cod

oil (if using) in a thin stream. Taste and season with salt
and freshly ground black pepper. Keep warm.

FISH
4 x 175 g (6 oz) fillets of cod, skinned and
any large bones removed with tweezers
salt and freshly ground pepper

To cook the fish
Pre-heat the oven to 220°C/425°F/gas mark 7.
Place the four fillets on a greased non-stick baking tray.
Season with salt and freshly ground black pepper.
Spread a thin layer of tapenade over the fish and bake in
the preheated oven for approximately 8-10 minutes.

To serve
Put a few spoonfuls of the ratatouille in the centre of four
warmed plates. Arrange a cod fillet on top of the
ratatouille. Finally, drizzle the yellow pepper coulis in a
thin line around this and serve immediately.

Daily catch, Kinsale

This small, cosy hotel, run by Brian and Ann Cronin, is located in the heart of Kinsale -
'Ireland's culinary capital' and is situated on the site of the old fish market. Their menu reflects
this access to outstanding local produce from some of the best fishing grounds in Europe.
Brian Cronin has had an important influence on the development of quality food in Kinsale.

bread and butter pudding
with crème anglaise

BREAD AND BUTTER PUDDING
1 loaf of brioche or,
500 g (1 lb) of left over
sponge or white bread
250 ml (8 fluid oz) milk
250 ml (8 fluid oz) cream
3 eggs
75 g (3 oz) sugar
zest of 1 orange
zest of 1 lemon

CRÈME ANGLAISE
250ml (8 fluid oz) cream
3 egg yolks
62g (2½ oz) sugar
1 vanilla pod (or 2-3 drops of vanilla
essence)

Pre-heat the oven to 180°C/350°F/gas mark 4.

Bread and butter pudding
In a bowl, put cream, milk, eggs, sugar and orange and lemon zest.
Mix together with a whisk until sugar is dissolved.
Cut either the brioche, sponge or white bread into cubes. For individual puddings, butter 4 ramekins, place the brioche (or sponge/white bread) into the ramekins. Pour in the egg mixture slowly until full to the top and cook in the oven for 15-20 minutes.

Crème anglaise
Mix together the egg yolks and sugar in a mixing bowl, using a whisk.
Bring the cream to the boil.
Add the cream to the egg mixture and whisk together. Return the mixture to a pan on a low heat, stirring constantly until it begins to thicken. When the mixture coats the back of a spoon, remove from the heat.
Leave to cool and then place in a clean container and store in the refrigerator until required.

To serve
Serve the pudding warm with the crème anglaise.

couscous cakes
with goat's cheese and mango salsa

SERVES 4

COUSCOUS CAKES
225 g (8 oz) couscous
500 ml (16 fluid oz) water
25 g (1 oz) butter
1 teaspoon salt

2 tablespoons of sunflower oil
2 onions peeled and finely chopped

2 eggs beaten
1 bunch of fresh parsley chopped
1 bunch of fresh mint, chopped
a few handfuls of semolina to mix

1 fresh soft Irish goat's cheese, sliced
(St. Tola, Croghan, Cais Chleire or St Macha)

MANGO SALSA
1 red pepper
50 ml (1¾ fluid oz) medium sherry
50 ml (2 fluid oz) water
50 ml (2 fluid oz) white wine vinegar
2 tablespoons of sugar
1 teaspoon of Chinese 5 spice
½ teaspoon salt
1 tablespoon of lemon juice
1 ripe mango, peeled and diced

Couscous cakes
Put the water, salt and butter into a medium sized saucepan and bring to the boil. When the butter has melted, add the couscous and mix well. Turn off the heat, cover with a lid and leave for at least five minutes.

Heat the oil in a heavy based frying pan. Add the onions and sauté gently until they are soft.

Beat the eggs in a large bowl, add the couscous, onions and herbs. Mix thoroughly with your hands, squishing the mixture through your fingers. Add one or two handfuls of semolina and mix until the mixture is sticky and firm enough to form cakes. If it is too sticky, add a little more semolina.
With wet hands form the mixture into 12 small cakes. Sprinkle some semolina onto a large plate or tray and sit the couscous cakes onto this. Chill in the refrigerator for at least half an hour.

To cook the couscous cakes
Preheat the oven to 180°C/350°F/gas mark 4.
Heat some oil in a large frying pan and fry the cakes briefly on each side until lightly golden. Put them onto a baking tray, place a slice of goat's cheese on top and bake in the preheated oven for about 15 minutes until the cheese has blistered and lightly browned.

Mango salsa
Put all the ingredients except the mango in a food processor. Process in an on/off method until the mixture is finely chopped. Remove to a bowl and add the diced mango. Mix well.

To serve
Place a few tablespoons of mango salsa in the centre of four plates. Arrange three cous couscakes around this and serve immediately.

This bright and spacious house has been created from what was once the more austere atmosphere of a convent. Con McLoughlin and Karen Austen serve delicous organic food (the vegetables are grown in their impressive walled garden), seven nights a week and for Sunday lunch.

roast pheasant
with apricot, port and balsamic sauce

SERVES 4

2 plump pheasants
salt and freshly ground black pepper
12-16 streaky rashers

SAUCE
1 litre (1¾ pints) home made fresh chicken stock
250 ml (8 fluid oz) red wine
100 ml (3 fluid oz) port wine
100 g (4 oz) dried apricots, chopped
1 tablespoon balsamic vinegar

Preheat the oven to 200°C/400°F/gas mark 6.

To cook the pheasant
Split each pheasant down the middle. Place them, breast side up, in a roasting tin. Season with salt and freshly ground black pepper and cover the skin of each section with the streaky rashers. Cook in the preheated oven for 15 minutes, turn the oven down to 150°C/300°F/gas mark 2 and cook for a further 15 minutes.

Sauce
Put the chicken stock into a medium-sized heavy saucepan.
Bring to the boil and reduce until about 250 ml (8 fluid oz) of liquid remains.

Put the red wine and port into a separate saucepan and bring this to the boil. Reduce again until about 100 ml (3 fluid oz) of this remains. Pour the reduced stock into the wine and port saucepan and stir in the apricots and the balsamic vinegar. Cook for another 5 minutes.

Taste and adjust the seasoning with salt and freshly ground black pepper.

To serve
Remove the bacon from the pheasant and discard. Place a portion of pheasant in the centre of four warmed plates.
Pour over the sauce and serve immediately.

rhubarb
crème brûlée

the restaurant is sited in a former convent

SERVES 4

500g (1 lb) young rhubarb
50 g (2 oz) white sugar
2 tablespoons grenadine
75 g (2¾ oz) caster sugar
5 egg yolks
450 ml (16 fluid oz) cream
½ vanilla pod, split
4 teaspoons of caster sugar for sprinkling

Rhubarb
Trim and rinse the rhubarb and chop into 2½ cm (1 in) pieces. Put into a saucepan with 50 g (2 oz) sugar, cover with a lid and cook gently, shaking the pan frequently until the rhubarb has softened. Remove from the heat and stir in the grenadine. Spoon the rhubarb into 4 ramekins.

Crème
Whisk the sugar with the egg yolks to thick ribbons. Heat the cream gently with the split vanilla pod. When the cream comes to the boil, whisk slowly onto the egg mix. Pour onto the rhubarb. Chill.

To serve
Sprinkle 1 teaspoon of caster sugar over each crème brûlée and brown with a blow torch or otherwise put under a grill.

Note: The Rhubarb Season.
Forced — December to March.
Main crop — March to June.
The best rhubarb is that which has been forced, and is thus thinner and more delicate.

pea and coriander soup

SERVES ABOUT 6

SOUP
55 g (2 oz) butter
140 g (5 oz) onion, finely chopped
2 cloves garlic, peeled and chopped
1 green chilli, de-seeded and finely chopped
450 g (1 lb) fresh peas
(good quality frozen ones are also fine)
900 ml (1½ pints) home-made chicken stock
about 2 tablespoons freshly chopped coriander
salt and freshly ground black pepper sugar

GARNISH
softly whipped cream
fresh coriander leaves

This utterly delicious soup has a perky zing with the addition of fresh chilli.

Melt the butter over a gentle heat and sweat the onion, garlic and chilli for 3-4 minutes.
Add the peas and cover with the stock.
Bring to the boil and simmer for 7-8 minutes.
Add the freshly chopped coriander and liquidise in a blender.
Season with salt and pepper and add a pinch of sugar, which enhances the flavour.

To serve
Serve with a swirl of softly whipped cream and a few fresh coriander leaves.

Herb Garden, Ballymaloe School

In 1970, Myrtle Allen's son Tim brought his wife Darina into the family business and in 1983 they established the cookery school at Kinoith, Shanagarry, just two miles from Ballymaloe House. It is now a highly regarded centre for residential cookery courses attracting international cooks and there are also shorter theme courses and gardening classes. In 1998 a cafe and shop was opened

sweet and sour pork
with prunes, raisins, pine kernels and polenta

"Jo Bettoja, whose food I adore, served us this rich sweet-sour stew in her home in Rome.
It is an old family recipe for wild boar that has been passed down through the generations. Timmy and I loved the rich gutsy flavour so she kindly shared her recipe with us." Darina Allen

SERVES 8-10

MARINADE
6 juniper berries
10 black peppercorns
2 bay leaves
½ teaspoon thyme leaves
1 carrot, chopped
1 onion, chopped
1 stick celery, chopped
725 ml (24 fl oz) or more dry red wine
50 ml (2 fluid oz) red wine vinegar

1.7 kg (4 lb) boneless shoulder
or leg of pork, cubed
5 tablespoons olive oil
sea salt
180 ml (6 fluid oz) red wine vinegar
freshly ground black pepper
36 prunes, soaked in water
55 g (2 oz) raisins, plumped in hot water
50 g (1¾ oz) pine nuts, toasted
2 tablespoons sugar
40 g (1½ oz) dark chocolate, grated

Mix all the ingredients for the marinade together in a bowl. Add the cubes of pork and stir well. Cover and marinate for 48 hours in the refrigerator. Stir every now and then during this period.

Preheat the oven to 160°C/325°F/gas mark 3.

Drain the meat and reserve the marinade and the vegetables. Dry the meat on kitchen paper. Heat 4 tablespoons of the olive oil in a frying pan on a high heat. Brown the meat on all sides and then transfer the pieces to a casserole and season with salt. Add a little more oil to the pan and cook the marinated vegetables for 10-15 minutes or until the onion is soft. Add a few tablespoons of the marinade to prevent the vegetables from burning. Add to the casserole. De-glaze the pan with the reserved marinade plus 50 ml (2 fluid oz) of the vinegar, bring to the boil and scrape into the casserole. Add ½ teaspoon freshly ground black pepper, cover the casserole and cook in the preheated oven until the meat is tender, about 1½ hours.

Remove the meat to a bowl and strain the sauce into a saucepan. Press the vegetables through the sieve to get the last of the juices. Add the prunes, raisins and pine nuts to the sauce.

In another small saucepan simmer the remaining red wine vinegar with 12 tablespoons sugar for 4 minutes, then add to the sauce with the chocolate and the meat. Bring to the boil slowly and simmer for 15 minutes. Taste and adjust the seasoning if necessary.

Serve with soft polenta and follow with a good green salad.

polenta

To accompany sweet and sour pork on previous page

"Polenta is a most adaptable dish. It can be served hot, the moment it is cooked, or it can be turned into a wet dish, rinsed in cold water and allowed to get cold. It can then be sliced and char-grilled, pan-grilled, toasted or fried and served with all sorts of toppings. It can even be cut into thin slices and layered with a sauce just like lasagne."

SERVES 6-8

1.7 litres (3 pints) water
2 teaspoons salt
225 g (8 oz) coarse polenta flour (maize)
115 g (4 oz) butter
85-115 g (3-4 oz) freshly grated parmesan
(Parmigiano Reggiano is best) (optional)
sea salt and freshly ground black pepper

Polenta
Put the water into a deep, heavy bottomed saucepan and bring to the boil. Add the salt, then sprinkle in the polenta flour very slowly, letting it slip gradually through your fingers, whisking all the time (this should take about 3-4 minutes). Bring to the boil and when it starts to 'erupt like a volcano' turn the heat down to the absolute minimum - it's best to use a heat diffuser mat if you have one. Cook for about 40 minutes, stirring regularly. I use a whisk at the beginning but as soon as the polenta comes to the boil I change to a flat bottomed wooden spoon. If you stir constantly on a slightly higher heat, the cooking time can be reduced to about 20 minutes, but the result is more digestible if cooked more slowly over a longer period. The polenta is cooked when it is very thick but not solid and comes away from the sides of the pot as you stir.
As soon as the polenta is cooked, stir in the butter, freshly grated parmesan and lots of pepper. Taste and add a little more sea salt if necessary. The polenta should be soft and flowing: if it is a little too stiff, add some boiling water. Serve immediately.

yoghurt and cardamom
with pomegranate seeds perfumed with rose blossom water

SERVES 8-10

YOGHURT AND CARDAMOM
¼ teaspoon green cardamom seeds, freshly ground
(you'll need about 8-10 cardamom pods depending on size)
230 ml (8 fluid oz) milk
175-200 g (6-7 oz) caster sugar
200 ml (7 fluid oz) cream
3 rounded teaspoons of powdered gelatine
425 ml (15 fluid oz) natural yoghurt

POMEGRANATE SEEDS WITH ROSE BLOSSOM WATER
6-8 pomegranates depending on size
a little lemon juice
1-2 tablespoons caster sugar
rose blossom water to taste

DECORATION
sweet geranium or mint leaves

Yoghurt and cardamom
Remove the seeds from the cardamom pods and crush in a pestle and mortar. Put the milk, sugar and cream into a stainless steel saucepan with the ground cardamom. Stir until the sugar has dissolved and the mixture is warm to the touch. Remove from the heat and leave to infuse while you dissolve the gelatine.
Put 3 tablespoons of cold water into a small bowl, sprinkle the gelatine over the water, and allow to sponge for a few minutes. Put the bowl into a saucepan of simmering water until the gelatine has melted and is completely clear. Add a little of the cardamom infused milk mixture, stir well and then mix this into the rest. Whisk the yoghurt lightly until smooth and creamy and stir into the cardamom mixture. Pour into a wide serving dish or a lightly oiled ring mould and leave to set for several hours.

Pomegranates
Cut the pomegranates in half around the 'equator'. Carefully separate the seeds from the membrane. Put the seeds into a bowl, sprinkle with just a little freshly squeezed lemon juice and add caster sugar and rose blossom water to taste. Put in the refrigerator until well chilled.

To serve
If the yoghurt and cardamom have been set in a ring mould, turn out on to a chilled plate. Fill the centre with chilled rose-scented pomegranate seeds. Decorate with sweet geranium or mint leave or even prettier, with crystallized rose petals.

Recipes reproduced by kind permission of Kyle Cathie Ltd. Taken from, *A Year at Ballymaloe Cookery School (1997)*, by Darina Allen.

fillet of turbot and crab with red peppercorns and butter sauce

In the Scilly area of Kinsale one of the longest serving and most popular restaurants in the region, Man Friday stands sentinel over the harbour and town. Owned and run by Philip and Joss Horgan since 1978 when it was acquired from Peter Barry, Man Friday has grown from its original snug restaurant around a bar, to its current layout, on four different levels.

a warm salad of goat's cheese,
roasted peppers, semi sundried tomatoes, olives and toasted hazelnuts

SERVES 4

CROSTINI
12 slices of French bread stick
extra virgin olive oil

ROASTED PEPPERS
1 red pepper
1 yellow pepper
1 green pepper
4 tablespoons of olive oil
salt and freshly ground pepper

FRENCH DRESSING
3 tablespoons of extra virgin olive oil
1 tablespoon of white wine vinegar
½ teaspoons of Dijon mustard,
salt and freshly ground black pepper

SALAD
mixed salad leaves
1½ tablespoons of pesto
24 pieces of semi-sundried tomatoes
24 black olives
toasted hazelnuts chopped
225 g (8 oz) goat's cheese

Crostini
Heat the olive oil in a pan. When hot, put in a few slices of French bread and cook until golden. Turn with tongs and cook until golden on the other side. Remove and drain on kitchen paper. Repeat until all the crostini are cooked.

Roasted peppers
Preheat the grill. Brush peppers with olive oil and grill until the skin darkens and begins to blister, and the flesh is soft. Remove to a bowl and cover with a plastic bag or cling film, and leave for 10-15 minutes as this will make them much easier to peel. Remove the skin, seeds and stalks from the peppers and divide each one into four pieces. Arrange the pepper slices on a plate and season with sea salt and freshly ground black pepper. Drizzle with some olive oil.

Dressing
Mix the oil and vinegar in a bowl, add the mustard, salt and freshly ground black pepper and whisk well. Toss the salad leaves with the dressing and divide between four plates.

To serve
Spread the goat's cheese on the crostini and grill until the cheese begins to bubble.
Arrange the sliced peppers, sundried tomatoes, olives, hazelnuts and pesto attractively on the salad leaves and place three crostini on each salad.
Serve immediately.

fillet of turbot and crab
with red peppercorns and butter sauce

SERVES 4

BUTTER SAUCE
4 tablespoons of dry white wine
2 tablespoons of white wine vinegar
50 g (2 oz) shallots,
peeled and finely chopped
a pinch of freshly ground pepper
2 tablespoons of cold water
200 g (7 oz) unsalted butter
2 teaspoons of red peppercorns
salt and lemon juice to taste

THE FISH
4 x 175 g (6 oz) fillets of turbot
salt and freshly ground pepper
a knob of butter
225 g (8 oz) fresh white crab meat

To make the butter sauce
Put the wine, wine vinegar, shallots and pepper into a heavy bottomed stainless steel saucepan. Bring to the boil, lower the heat and reduce until you have about 1 tablespoon of liquid left. Add the cold water and over a gentle heat whisk in the cold butter, in little pieces until completely absorbed. Strain through a fine sieve into a clean saucepan and reheat. Add the red peppercorns, season to taste with salt and lemon juice and keep warm in a bowl over hot but not simmering water.

To cook the fish
Heat the grill pan. Season the turbot fillets with salt and pepper and cook on the grill pan for approximately 30 seconds on each side. Remove to a heated plate and keep warm.
In a separate pan, melt the knob of butter, add the crab meat and heat through gently.

To serve
Spoon a little of the butter and peppercorn sauce onto four hot plates, arrange a turbot fillet and some crab meat on top of the sauce.
Serve immediately.

miso soup

FOR 1 LITRE OF SOUP

2 tablespoons of sesame seed oil
4 medium onions quartered
3 carrots thickly sliced
2 leeks, white part only, thinly sliced
3 shallots, un-peeled, cut in quarters
1 large piece of root ginger, peeled,
broken and crushed
1 bulb of garlic
2 bay leaves
handful of dried shiitake mushrooms
(and/or porcini mushrooms)
boquet garni
(sage, parsley stalks, rosemary, coriander
tied together with string)
1 - 2 tablespoons of red wine vinegar
1 - 2 tablespoons of soya sauce
1 litre (1¾ pints) vegetable stock
freshly ground Sichuan
peppercorns to taste

1 - 2 teaspoons/tablespoons
(according to taste) of Mugi miso

GARNISH
a bunch of fresh chives finely chopped
15g (½ oz) seaweed,
such as Hijiki or Arame

The number of ways to prepare a good miso soup is, perhaps, as many as there are cooks. Miso soup can change in flavour as you change or vary the combination of vegetables. However, it is better to use strong flavoured vegetables, especially root vegetables.

Heat the sesame oil in a large heavy based saucepan. Add all the vegetables and toss them in the oil. Cook over a moderate heat until golden brown. (It is important to allow the vegetables to get really brown as this adds to the dark colour and the main taste of the miso soup later.)

Add the red wine vinegar and the soya sauce. Cover the vegetables with vegetable stock, add the bay leaves and the bunch of herbs and bring to the boil. Reduce the heat and simmer gently for 1 hour.

Remove the bay leaves and the bouquet garni and press the liquid and vegetables through a very fine sieve into a clean pan. Bring to the boil and remove from the heat. Mix in the Mugi miso. Do not allow the miso to boil. Taste and adjust the seasoning, adding a little of the crushed Sichuan peppercorns or freshly ground black pepper if you wish.

To serve
Serve immediately, sprinkled with chopped chives or spring onions, and perhaps some seaweed such as Hijiki or Arame.

Notes
Mugi miso is a dark fermented barley and soya bean paste.

Hijiki is sold coarsely shredded and has a sweet delicate flavour. It is an outstanding source of iron and calcium. Soak in boiling water for 20 minutes. Drain, then cover with fresh cold water, bring to the boil and simmer gently until tender - about 20 minutes. Drain and use as required.

Arame is a delicately flavoured seaweed which is cut into long thin strips after harvesting. It needs only 5 minutes soaking followed by 20 minutes cooking, as above, before use.

West Cork

baked fillet of john dory with courgette scales

SERVES 4

450 g (1 lb) courgettes
salt

4 x 150 g (5 oz) John Dory fillets
(leave the skin on and
remove any small bones
using a pliers or tweezers)

MARINADE
juice of 1 lime
65 ml (2½ fluid oz) extra virgin olive oil
a pinch of each of the following:
freshly ground Sichuan pepper
freshly ground coriander seeds
herbal salt

SAUCE
bones and head of the John Dory
25 g (1 oz) margarine
1 medium onion, peeled and finely chopped
1 large carrot, peeled and sliced
2 stalks of celery, sliced
1 glass of dry white wine
575 ml (1 pint) approx. cold water
1 broken bay leaf
2 fresh parsley stalks

GARNISH
2 tomatoes, peeled,
de-seeded and cut into concassé
1 tablespoon of freshly chopped tarragon

Courgettes
Using a sharp knife slice the courgettes as thinly as possible about 5 mm (1/4 in). Season them lightly with salt, cover with a damp cloth and allow to stand for 20 minutes until the water oozes out of the tissues, then pat them dry.

Marinade
Mix together all the marinade ingredients and pour over the fillets. Seal with cling film and marinate for at least 2 hours in the refrigerator.

Sauce
Remove the gills from the fish head (their bitter flavour would spoil the stock) and wash the bones and head in several changes of cold water. Drain them and chop them roughly. Melt the margarine in a large saucepan. Stir in the vegetables and sweat over a low heat for 2-3 minutes, until they are soft but not coloured. Add the bones and cook for a further 2-3 minutes. Pour in the wine, increase the heat and boil to reduce the wine by half. Pour in just enough cold water to cover the bones, and add the herbs. Bring to the boil and adjust the heat to give a gentle simmer. Simmer, uncovered, for 20 minutes, skimming when necessary. Strain through a muslin-lined sieve into a clean saucepan. Return to the heat, bring to the boil and reduce slowly until you have only a quarter of the volume of liquid left. At this point the sauce should be just thick enough to form a film on the back of a spoon. Taste, and season with salt and freshly ground black pepper. Finish the sauce by stirring in the diced tomato and the chopped tarragon. Keep warm.

To cook the fish
Preheat the oven to 180°C/350°F/gas mark 4.
Place the fish fillets, skin side down, on a lightly oiled baking sheet. Arrange the courgette slices on top of the fillets, overlapping them slightly to give the effect of fish scales. Season with salt and freshly ground pepper. Bake in the preheated oven for approximately 7 minutes, or until the fillets are cooked and firm to the touch.

To serve
Carefully turn the fillets on to warmed plates and surround with the sauce. Serve immediately.

baked fillet of john dory with courgette scales

This Victorian house is surrounded by 40 acres of gardens and has been renovated to offer a fashionable blend of minimalism and luxury. Mirroring this philosophy, the cuisine also promotes a positive experience of nature, health and good taste.

strudel with a filling of butternut pumpkin and garden herbs
served with a red pepper coulis

SERVES 4

STRUDEL PASTRY
200 g (7 oz) plain white flour
1 teaspoon of salt
1 egg lightly beaten
1 tablespoon of vegetable oil
100 ml (3½ fluid oz) of warm water

FILLING
675g (1½ lb) pumpkin halved and seeded
2 shallots, peeled and finely chopped
1 tablespoon of vegetable oil
2 tablespoons of finely chopped fresh herbs (parsley, thyme, sage)
1 piece of root ginger 2.5 cm (1 in) peeled and finely minced
salt and freshly ground Sichuan peppercorns to taste

TO ASSEMBLE
white flour
1 egg yolk, beaten

Pastry
Sift the flour and salt into a mixing bowl. Combine the egg, water and oil in a separate bowl and beat well. Gradually add the water mixture and mix well to make a soft dough. Knead on a floured board until the pastry becomes smooth and elastic and no longer sticky. Cover with a warmed tight fitting bowl and leave at room temperature for 30-60 minutes.

Filling
Grate the de-seeded pumpkin with the coarse side of a stainless steel grater.
Heat the vegetable oil in a large pan over a moderate heat and sauté the shallots until they are soft and transparent. Add the pumpkin and cook until soft. Remove the pan from the heat and stir in the chopped mixed herbs. Season to taste with the grated ginger, salt and freshly ground Sichuan peppercorns. Leave to cool.

To assemble
Preheat the oven to 200°C/400°F/gas mark 6.
The strudel dough has to be stretched as wide as possible. Best would be to have two people working on this. It is perfect if you can read a newspaper through the dough!!
Cover a large table with a floured cloth and lay the pastry on the cloth. Gently pull and stretch the dough, placing both hands under it and pulling until it is paper thin.
Cut into a rectangle shape and spread the pumpkin filling in the lower third of the pastry. Fold over and then roll up like a Swiss roll with the help of the cloth. Remove the cloth, place on a lightly oiled baking tray and brush with the beaten egg yolk. Bake in the preheated oven for approximately 30 minutes until the strudel is golden brown and crisp.

COULIS

4 ripe red peppers, de-seeded and diced
2 shallots, peeled and finely chopped
1 tablespoon of olive oil
1 clove of garlic, unpeeled and broken
1 piece of root ginger 2.5 cm (1 in)
peeled and broken
120 ml (4 fluid oz) fresh vegetable stock
herbal salt and freshly ground pepper

GARNISH

½ red pepper, peeled and cut into dice
1 bunch of flat leaf parsley

Coulis

Heat the olive oil in a pan, put in the shallots and sweat over a gentle heat until soft. Add the chopped peppers, the clove of garlic and the ginger and cook for a further two minutes. Pour in the vegetable stock, bring to the boil, reduce the heat and simmer for 15 minutes. Remove the clove of garlic and the ginger and discard.

Pour into a liquidiser and blend until you have a light sauce consistency. Push the mixture through a fine sieve into a clean saucepan.

Reheat, taste and adjust seasoning with herbal salt and freshly ground pepper and keep warm.

To serve

Cut the strudel into 8 medium sized slices.

Spoon a little of the red pepper coulis into the centre of four warmed plates and arrange two slices of strudel, with edges overlapping, on top of the coulis. Scatter some diced red pepper on the sauce surrounding the strudel and decorate with a sprig of flat leaf parsley. Serve immediately.

roaring water deep sea scallops,
fresh watercress beurre blanc, and julienne of deep fried leek

SERVES 4

Scallops are at their best during the months from October to February

BEURRE BLANC SAUCE
a handful of watercress
1 teaspoon of white wine vinegar
2 teaspoons of white wine
2 shallots, peeled and very finely chopped
1 teaspoon of double cream
250 g (9 oz) unsalted butter, diced

Beurre blanc sauce
Wash and dry the watercress and remove the thicker stalks. Process in a blender, adding sufficient cold water to give a thick 'soup'. Remove to a bowl and reserve. Put the vinegar, wine vinegar and shallots into a small stainless steel saucepan, bring to the boil and reduce the liquid to a tablespoon. Add the double cream and boil again to reduce by one third.
Remove from the heat and whisk in the cold diced butter, a little at a time until the sauce has emulsified. Stir in the purée of fresh watercress and season to taste with salt and freshly ground pepper. Keep the sauce warm by pouring it into a stainless steel jug and sitting this in a bowl of boiling water.

SCALLOPS
12 whole fresh scallops
2 tablespoons of extra virgin olive oil

Scallops
Wash the scallops well, leaving the coral intact, and leave to dry on kitchen paper.
Preheat the grill.
Heat the olive oil in a heavy based frying pan until it begins to smoke. Season the scallops with salt and freshly ground pepper and add to the pan. Cook briefly for about 30 seconds on each side, turning only once. Finish cooking under the hot grill for 2-3 minutes.

GARNISH
75 g (3 oz) fresh leek, cut into fine julienne strips
4 teaspoons of corn flour
vegetable oil for deep-frying

Garnish
Preheat the oil in a deep fryer to 200°C/400°F/gas mark 6. Meanwhile, roll the julienne of leek in the corn flour, shake off the excess and deep fry until crisp and golden brown. Leave to drain on kitchen paper.

To serve
Place three scallops in the centre of four warmed plates. Spoon the watercress beurre blanc around the outside of the scallops and garnish with the julienne of leek.

the kitchen at the waterside inn

Specialising in seafood and steaks, the Waterside Inn
has been in business since 1996 and is run by
Thomas Brosnan in the premises formerly occupied
by the Black Sheep restaurant and pub.

supreme of chicken cordon bleu
roast breast of chicken stuffed with honey baked ham, smoked gubeen cheese, served with a wholegrain mustard sauce

SERVES 4

CHICKEN
2 fresh free-range
legless chickens
1 tablespoon of olive oil
a knob of butter

STUFFING
4 thin slices of honey
baked ham
4 slices of smoked
Gubeen cheese

SAUCE
275 ml (½ pint) of fresh
chicken stock
4 tablespoons of
wholegrain mustard
75 ml (2½ fluid oz)
fresh cream
15g (½ oz) butter
salt and freshly ground
black pepper

hot creamy mashed potato
(make in the usual way with)
900 g (2 lb) 'old' potatoes
150 ml (¼ pint) creamy milk
30-55 g (1-2 oz) butter
salt and freshly ground
pepper to taste

To prepare the supremes
With a sharp knife cut against the ridge of the breastbone to loosen the flesh from the bone. Disjoint the wing where it joins the carcass and continue down along the rib cage until the meat from one side of the breast separates from the bone in one piece.
Repeat the process for the all the supremes.
Remove the skin from the breasts and wings, and remove all the flesh from the wings. Only the bone of the wings should remain.
Slice the supremes of chicken lengthways to make a pocket for the stuffing.
Wrap each slice of cheese with a slice of ham and insert a parcel into each pocket in the chicken.

To cook the chicken
Preheat the oven to 200°C/400°F/gas mark 6.
Season the chicken with salt and freshly ground black pepper.
Heat some olive oil and a knob of butter in a frying pan until quite hot. Cook the chicken supremes until they are golden brown on both sides. Transfer to a baking sheet and place in the preheated oven for 12-15 minutes.
When cooked, remove from the oven and leave to rest for approximately 8 minutes before serving.

Sauce
Put the chicken stock in a heavy based saucepan, bring to the boil and reduce slightly.
Add the wholegrain mustard and the cream and boil again until the sauce reduces to a consistency thick enough to coat the back of a spoon.
Add any juices that have escaped from the chicken.
Remove from the heat and whisk in the cold butter, a little at a time.
Season to taste with salt and freshly ground black pepper.

To serve
Pipe some creamy hot mashed potato into the centre of four warmed plates. Arrange a supreme of chicken on

supreme of chicken cordon bleu

TO GARNISH
1 bunch of French parsley
2 small courgettes, turned
2 medium carrots, turned

top of the potato and carefully spoon the sauce around the outside of the plate.

Garnish with a sprig of French parsley and serve with turned carrot and courgettes.

Note: To turn the carrots and courgettes.
Peel the vegetables and cut into 5 cm (2 in) lengths. Stand each piece on end and slice lengthways into four. With a small sharp knife, trim each piece into a barrel or olive shape.
Cook in boiling salted water until tender but firm.
Use as a garnish for the chicken dish.

151

cork city

Arbutus Lodge Hotel
Montenotte
Cork City
021 501237
Declan & Patsy Ryan
Head Chef: Eric Theze

Café Paradiso
16 Lancaster Quay
Cork City
021 277939
Denis & Bridget Cotter

The Crawford Gallery Café
Crawford Art Gallery
Emmet Place
Cork City
021 274415
Chris O'Brien

Farmgate Café
Old English Market
Princess St.
Cork City
021 278134
Kay Harte

Fleming's
Silver Grange House
Tivoli
Cork City
021 821621
Michael & Eileen Fleming

Gingerbread House
10 Paul St.
Cork City
021 276411
Barnaby Blacker

Hayfield Manor Hotel
Perrot Avenue
College Rd
Cork City
021 315600
Manager: Ewan Plenderleith
Head Chef: Robert Cowley

Iago
42 English Market
Delacy Lane
Cork City
021 277047
Sean Calder-Potts

Issacs
48 McCurtain St
Cork City
021 500011
Canice Sharkey
Catherine & Michael Ryan

Ivory Tower
The Exchange Buildings
35 Princes St.
Cork City
021 274665
Seamus O'Connell

Jacques
9 Phoenix St.
Cork City
021 277387
Jacque & Eithne Barry

Lovett's
Churchyard Lane
Well Road, Douglas
Cork City
021 294909
Lovett Family
Head Chef: Marie Harding

Michael's
71 Patrick St.
Cork City
021 277716
Michael Clifford

cork county

Adele's
Main St.
Schull
Co. Cork
028 28459
Adele & Simon Connor

Annie's
Main St.
Ballydehob
Co. Cork
028 37292
Annie Barry

Assolas Country House
Kanturk
Co. Cork
029 50015
Joe & Hazel Bourke

Ballymaloe Cookery School
Kinoith House
Shanagarry
Co. Cork
021 646785
Darina & Tim Allen

Ballymaloe House
Shanagarry
Co. Cork
021 652531
Myrtle Allen
Head Chef: Rory O'Connell

Blue Haven Hotel
Pearse St.
Kinsale
Co. Cork
021 772209
Brian Cronin
Head Chef: Peter Wood

Clean Slate
Midleton
Co. Cork
021 633655
Colm Falvey

Dunworley Cottage Restaurant
Dunworley
Butlerstown
Co. Cork
023 40314
Katherine Norén

Farmgate
Coolbawn
Midleton
Co. Cork
021 632771
Máróg O'Brien

Gregory's
Main St.
Carrigaline
Co. Cork
021 371512
Greg Dawson

Island Cottage
Heir Island
Nr. Skibbereen
Co. Cork
028 38102
John Desmond
Ellmarie Fenton

Lettercollum House
Timoleague
Co. Cork
023 46251
Con McLoughlin
Karen Austin

Liss Ard Lake Lodge
Skibbereen
Co. Cork
028 22365
Claudia Meister

Longueville House
Mallow
Co. Cork
022 47156
William & Aisling O'Callaghan

Man Friday
Scilly
Nr. Kinsale
Co. Cork
021 772260
Phillip Horgan

The Oystercatcher
Oysterhaven
Nr. Kinsale
Co. Cork
021 770822
Sylvia & Bill Patterson

The Waterside Inn
Main St.
Schull
Co. Cork
028 28203
Thomas Brosnan

index of recipe types

illustrations in italics

Pearl Barley and Mushrooms (Michael's) 23, *24*
Grilled Lamb Steak with Carmelised Shallots and
  Champ (Isaac's) 50
Loin of Lamb Roasted and Glazed with Honey,
  Mustard and Baked Shallots in Sea Salt and
  Balsamic Syrup (Arbutus Lodge Hotel) 68
Dunworley Cottage Pork in Calvados Marinade
  (Dunworley Cottage) 85
Sweet - Sour Pork with Prunes, Raisins, Pine Kernels
  and Polenta (Ballymaloe Cookery School) 134
Tripe and Drisheen from the English Market
  (Farmgate Café) 74

Pasta
Angel Hair Pasta with Artichokes, Sundried
  Tomatoes and Chilli (Adele's) 104, *105*
Marinated Wild Mushrooms with Asparagus on
  Fresh Linguini and Pesto
  (Hayfield Manor Hotel) 52
Penne with Red Pepper Sauce, Cream Cheese and
  Scallions (Isaac's) 48, *49*
Tagliatelle with Asparagus, Cream and Parmesan
  (Isaacs) 47

Vegetarian Dishes
Angel Hair Pasta with Artichokes, Sundried
  Tomatoes and Chilli (Adele's) 104, *105*
Aubergine, Tomato, Olive and Goat's Cheese
  Galette, with a Balsamic Tomato Vinaigrette
  (Café Paradiso) 19, *16*
Cous Cous Cakes with Goat's Cheese and Mango
  Salsa (Lettercollum House) 130
Marinated Wild Mushrooms with Asparagus on Fresh
  Linguini and Pesto (Hayfield Manor Hotel) 52
Penne with Red Pepper Sauce, Cream Cheese and
  Scallions (Isaac's) 48, *49*
Spinach and Mushroom Pancake (Crawford Café)
  26, *27*
Strudel with a filling of Butternut Pumpkin and
  Garden Herbs served with a Pepper Coulis
  (Liss Ard Lake Lodge) 146
Tagliatelle with Asparagus, Cream and Parmesan
  (Isaacs) 47
Vegetable Ragout (Island Cottage) 116

Salads
A Warm Salad of Goats Cheese, Roasted Peppers,
  Semi-Sundried Tomatoes, Olives and Toasted
  Hazelnuts (Man Friday) 141
Broad Bean, New Potato and Roasted Beetroot Salad
  with a Walnut Dressing and Orla Shavings
  (Café Pardiso) 18
Mango Salsa (Lettercollum House) 130
Green Salad (Ballymaloe House) 86

Vegetable Side-Dishes
Caramelised Shallots (Isaacs) 48
Carrot and Orange Purée (Island Cottage) 118

Champ (Isaac's) 48
Champ (Jacques) 62
Colcannon (Jacques) 62
Fantailed Potatoes with Rosemary and Garlic
  (Crawford Café) 27
Green Salad (Ballymaloe House) 86
Green Salsa (Farmgate) 79
Mango Salsa (Lettercollum House) 130
Olive Oil Mash (Jacques) 62
Red Cabbage (Crawford Café) 26
Red Onion Marmalade (Michael's) 22
Roast Potatoes (Island Cottage) 118
Stir Fried Greens (Jacques) 63
Vegetable Ragout (Island Cottage) 116

Vinaigrettes and Butters
Anchovy Butter (Jacques) 60
Balsamic Tomato Vinaigrette (Café Paradiso) 18
Lemon Vinaigrette (Longueville House) 122
Mustard Butter (Jacques) 60
Tomato and Chive Dressing (Lovetts) 36
Tomato Vinaigrette (Jacques) 60

Desserts
A Dark Chocolate Marquise wrapped in a Jacquard
  Sponge with Toasted Coconut and Kirsh
  Blackberries (The Clean Slate) 97
Bread and Butter Pudding with Creme Anglaise
  (Blue Haven) 129
Crushed Blueberries and Cream
  (Ballymaloe House) 88
Elderflower Sorbet (Dunworley Cottage) 85
Fresh Orange Souffle (Annie's) 103
Gooseberry - Almond Tartlets with an Amaretto
  Custard (Café Paradiso) 20
Grandma's Christmas Cake
  (Gingerbread House) 42
Hot Ice Cream Crackers with an Orange Coulis
  (Orange and Poppy Seed Ice Cream, wrapped in Filo
  Pastry, shaped into a Cracker and deep fried)
  (Lovetts) 38, *39*
Iced Coffee and Praline Parfait with Irish Coffee
  Sauce (Gregory's Restaurant) 115, *114*
Lemon Cake (Adele's) 107
Peach Melba (Baked peaches in red wine,
  mascarapone cream and iced strawberry mousse)
  (Jacques) 64, *65*
Queen of Puddings (Farmgate) 76
Rhubarb Creme Brulee (Lettercollum House) 133
Rich Chocolate and Nut Cake (Assolas House) 92
Strawberries Au Gratin flavoured with Baileys
  (Arbutus Lodge Hotel) 69
Strawberry Tarts (Gingerbread House) 44, *42*
Tarte Au Citron (Flemings) 58, *59*
Yogurt and Cardamon with Pomegranate Seeds
  perfumed with Rose Blossom Water
  (Ballymaloe Cookery School) 137

index of ingredients

illustrations in italics

Red Peppercorn and Butter
Sauce (Man Friday) 140
Fresh Crab Cakes
(Gregory's Restaurant) 112

Custard
Gooseberry - Almond Tartlets
with an Amaretto Custard
(Café Paradiso) 20

Duck Breast with a Lemon Sauce,
Lemon Confit, Roast
Potatoes,Carrot and Orange
Purée (Island Cottage) 118

Elderflower Sorbet
(Dunworley Cottage) 85

French Beans
Monkfish Pan Fried in Garlic,
Chilli and Fresh Ginger on a Bed
of Blackened French Beans
(The Clean Slate) 96

Gooseberry - Almond Tartlets with
an Amaretto Custard
(Café Paradiso) 20

Hake
Baked Silver Hake on Crispy
Noodles with a Bacon and
Thyme Butter Sauce (Lovetts) 37

Ham
Roast Supreme of Chicken
stuffed with Honey Baked Ham
and Smoked Gubeen Cheese,
served with a Wholegrain
Mustard Sauce
(The Waterside Inn) 150,*151*

Ice Cream
Hot Ice cream Crackers with an
Orange Coulis Iced Coffee and
Praline Parfait with Irish Coffee
Sauce (Gregory's Restaurant)
38,*39*

John Dory
Baked Fillet of John Dory with
Courgette Scales
(Liss Ard Lake Lodge) 142,*143*

Lamb
Grilled Lamb Steak with
Carmelised Shallots and Champ
(Isaac's) 50
Loin of Lamb Roasted and
Glazed with Honey, Mustard and
Baked Shallots in Sea Salt and
Balsamic Syrup
(Arbutus Lodge Hotel) 68
Sauteed Lamb's Tongues on a
Wholegrain Mustard Mash with
tossed Rocket Leaves
(The Clean Slate) 94,*95*

Leek
Roaring Water Deep Sea Scallops,
Fresh Watercress Beurre Blanc,
Julienne of Deep Fried Leek
(The Waterside Inn) 148

Lemon
Breast of Chicken marinated with
Lemon, Garlic and Chilli and
served with a White Wine and
Basil Sauce
(Gregory's Restaurant) 113
Duck Breast with a Lemon Sauce,
Lemon Confit, Roast Potatoes,
Carrot and Orange Purée
(Island Cottage) 118
Lemon Cake (Adele's) 107
Lemon Vinaigrette
(Longueville House) 122
Pan Fried Monkfish with a Tangy
Lemon Sauce (Annie's) 100
Tarte Au Citron (Flemmings)
58,*59*

Lentils
Pan Fried Cod with Puy Lentils
and Green Salsa (Farmgate)
81,*80*

Mackarel with Herbs and
Mushrooms, and Green Salad
(Ballymaloe House) 86,*87*

Mango
Couscous Cakes with Goats
Cheese and Mango Salsa
(Lettercollum House) 130

Miso
Miso Soup
(Liss Ard Lake Lodge) 144

Monkfish
Monkfish Pan Fried in Garlic,
Chilli and Fresh Ginger on a Bed
of Blackened French Beans
(The Clean Slate) 96
Pan Fried Monkfish with a Tangy
Lemon Sauce (Annie's) 100

Mushrooms
Clonakilty Black Pudding with a
Stew of Wild Rice, Pearl Barley
and Mushrooms
(Michael's) 23,*24*
Mackarel with Herbs and
Mushrooms, and Green Salad
Marinated Wild Mushrooms with
Asparagus on Fresh Linguini and
Pesto
(Hayfield Manor Hotel) 52
Spinach and Mushroom Pancake
(Crawford Café) 26,*27*

Mussels Gratinated with Herb

Breadcrumbs and served with a
Vierge Sauce
(Longueville House) 124,*125*

Mustard Butter (Jacques) 60

Nettle Soup
(Dunworley Cottage) 84

Onions
Deep Fried Chicken with
Mileen's Cheese on Red Onion
Marmalade (Cliffords) 22
Grilled Lamb Steak with
Carmelised Shallots and Champ
(Isaac's) 50
Loin of Lamb Roasted and
Glazed with Honey, Mustard and
Baked Shallots in Sea Salt and
Balsamic Syrup
(Arbutus Lodge Hotel) 68

Orange
Fresh Orange Souffle
(Annie's) 103
Hot Ice Cream Crackers with an
Orange Coulis (Lovetts) 38,*39*

Oysters
Irish Rock Oysters with Angel
hair Pasta and a Chilli, Garlic and
Oyster Sauce (Oystercatcher) 108

Pancakes
Spinach and Mushroom Pancake
(Crawford Café) 26,*27*

Peas
Pea and Coriander Soup with
Chilli
(Ballymaloe Cookery School) 136

Peach Melba
(Baked Peaches in Red Wine,
Mascarapone Cream and Iced
Strawberry Mousse) (Jacques) 76

Peppers
Escallop of Roasted Seafresh Cod
with a Sundried Tapenade Crust
on a Bed of Orange and Caper
Ratatouille with Roasted Yellow
Pepper Coulis (Blue Haven)
126,*127*
Penne with Red Pepper Sauce,
Cream Cheese and Scallions
(Isaac's) 48,*46*
Strudel with a filling of Butternut
Pumpkin and Garden Herbs,
served with a Pepper Coulis
(Liss Ard Lake Lodge) 146

Pesto
Basil Pesto (Adele's) 104,*105*
Mushrooms with Asparagus on
Fresh Linguini and Pesto
(Hayfield Manor Hotel) 52

index